The Question of HAMLET

BY HARRY LEVIN

D0096235

New York
THE VIKING PRESS

COPYRIGHT © 1959 BY OXFORD UNIVERSITY PRESS, INC.

COMPASS BOOKS EDITION
ISSUED IN 1961 BY THE VIKING PRESS, INC.
625 MADISON AVENUE, NEW YORK 22, N.Y.

DISTRIBUTED IN CANADA BY
THE MACMILLAN COMPANY OF CANADA LIMITED

SECOND PRINTING AUGUST 1964

THIS EDITION PUBLISHED BY ARRANGEMENT WITH
OXFORD UNIVERSITY PRESS, INC.

PRINTED IN THE U.S.A. BY THE MURRAY PRINTING CO.

For MARINA

PREFACE

PREFACE

THe core of this little book consists, with slight modifications and amplifications, of the Alexander Lectures as presented at the University of Toronto on March 18, 19, and 20, 1958. To the authorities of University College and especially to the head of the English Department, Professor A. S. P. Woodhouse, I feel profoundly indebted for the gracious hospitality with which these ideas and their proponent were entertained. Because the three successive lectures—now chapters—were directed toward a close rereading of the play as a whole, relating its style and structure to other aspects more frequently discussed by scholars and critics, I have ventured to indicate some of the general points from which this interpretation takes its departure in my opening statement of presuppositions. By way of supplementation, I have appended three briefer and more specialized studies in *Hamlet*-problems, dealing with some particularities of theatrical convention, ethical argument, and *explication de texte*. They are reprinted, substantially as first published: the article on 'the antic disposition' from the *Shakespeare Jahrbuch*, XCIV (1958), the review of *Hamlet: Father and Son* from the *Shakespeare Quarterly*, VII, 1 (Winter, 1956), and the explication of the Player's speech from *The Kenyon Review*, XII, 2 (Spring, 1950). To the editors of those publications, I would express my thanks.

Though I have tried to make specific acknowledgements where-ever they may be due, no one who is incautious enough to write anything about *Hamlet* can honestly say just how much he owes—or what, if anything, he does not owe—to the many previous writers on the subject. I can only say that I have taken advantage of the cumulative discussion, of which the outlines are traced by the Furness Variorum Edition, the *Hamlet Bibliography* of A. A. Raven (Chicago, 1936), the ninth volume of the *Shakespeare Survey*, and therein notably 'Studies in *Hamlet*, 1901–1955' by Clifford Leech. Nor should I fail to acknowledge how often the spoken word—from the lips of actors, teachers, colleagues, or students—tends to affect one's own impressions of a work so endlessly debatable. The text from which I quote, and to which I would constantly refer the reader, is the annotated edition of George Lyman Kittredge (Boston, 1939). However, I have parted from my revered teacher, and followed a prevailing trend among later editors and commentators, in one particular reading: 'sullied' for 'solid' in the first line of Hamlet's First Soliloquy. Because the soliloquies are most conveniently designated by their numerical sequence, and because certain episodes are conventionally referred to by certain names, it may facilitate cross-reference to have at hand the following tabulations:

First Soliloquy: I. ii. 129–59

Second Soliloquy: I. v. 92–112

Third Soliloquy: II. ii. 575–673

Fourth Soliloquy: III. i. 56–88

Fifth Soliloquy: III. ii. 406–17

Sixth Soliloquy: III. iii. 73–96

Seventh Soliloquy: IV. iv. 37–66

Council Scene: I. ii. 1–128

Fishmonger Scene: II. ii. 171–224

Schoolfellow Scene: II. ii. 225–385

Nunnery Scene: III. i. 88–169

Play Scene: III. ii. 95–281

Prayer Scene: III. iii. 36–98

Closet Scene: III. iv. 1–52

Portrait Scene: III. iv. 53–217

Graveyard Scene: V. i: 1–245

Cambridge, Massachusetts
April 23, 1958

H. L.

CONTENTS

THE QUESTION OF HAMLET

PRESUPPOSITIONS

WHen Hamlet points out a cloud to Polonius, he points the way that criticism has taken. Polonius, with his hyphenated categories, his readiness to crack the wind of a poor phrase, his objection to certain adjectives and his fondness for others, is a typical critic. His response to what might be called Hamlet's ink-blot test—his agreement that the cloud resembles now a weasel, then a camel, and again a whale—succinctly foreshadows the process of interpreting the play. For there can be no doubt that it has clouded our mental horizons with its peculiar sense of obscurity or of anxiety, and has inspired its interpreters to discern an unending succession of shapes. It is quite probable that no other play has ever been so fully discussed or so frequently acted. And if, as Charles Lamb reminds us, every actor has aspired to the titular part, then perhaps any professor of English literature may be forgiven for presuming to set down a few comments of his own. Obviously, no single commentary could pretend to encompass the subject at this stage, or to decide once for all between alternatives which are conditioned to provoke further debate. *Hamlet*, like the major problems of human experience, has been surrounded with a whole library. Over the sixty-year period following the two-volume Variorum Edition of 1877, and covered by the *Hamlet Bibliography* of A. A. Raven, it is computed that twelve days have not passed without witnessing the publication of some additional item of Hamletiana. Current listings would seem to show that this rate of incidence has not declined; on the contrary, there seems to be an increase in the number of monographic studies concentrating on *Hamlet*, such as the present undertaking.

One is released, by these very circumstances, from the obligation to be definitive or, on the other hand, from the endeavor to be wholly original. One is also obliged by them to acknowledge a comprehensive, though not always conscious, debt to innumerable predecessors, to all of those who have engaged in the argument up to the point at which we enter it. So much has already been said, so many extremes have been reached, that we cannot do much further harm. Can we add anything helpful to the discussion? 'Who is as the wise man?' asked Hamlet's skeptical predecessor, the preacher of Ecclesiastes, 'and who knoweth the interpretation of a thing?' A question not to be answered with undue facility. We shall be dealing, as we had better recognize, with the most problematic of problem plays. It has been described, in varying terms, as a poetic puzzle, as a dramatic sphinx, and as the Mona Lisa of literature. This has led most of its commentators to read it as if it were some sort of riddle—as if, by somehow plucking the heart of Hamlet's mystery, we should come to know what God and man is. Yet Hamlet expressly warns against such an approach, and keeps suggesting that there are reaches of thought which cannot be spanned by naturalistic or academic solutions. Insofar as he is concerned with knowledge, that is rather the object of a continuing quest than the substance of a final revelation. Thus an enigmatic atmosphere is of the essence, and we do more wisely to respect it than to explain it away. The tragedy may well include, among other things, the elements of a murder-mystery; but the suspense, in this case, does not end with the murderer's detection or indeed with the murdered man's revenge.

Philosophy, though it claims Hamlet's abiding concern, does not provide us with any key to his universe. Those who look for keys in a work of art have therefore tended to shift their ground to psychology. They have examined and re-examined the protagonist, diagnosing his melancholia and even treating him as the madman he feigns. With an unconscionable amount of casuistry, they have searched for motives between the lines and behind the scenes, divorcing his character from its context and moralizing over it. Now *Hamlet* without Hamlet would, of course, be altogether unthinkable; but Hamlet without *Hamlet* has been thought about all too much. The Prince of Denmark has been identified with many other personalities, none of them bearing much resemblance to any of the others. Gatherers of topical allusions have framed his portrait as that of James I, or else the Earl of Essex, or possibly Giordano Bruno. Imaginative writers have re-created him in the autobiographical image of a Wilhelm Meister or a Stephen Dedalus. The romantic legend of a weakling, too delicate for this world, culminated in the logical inference that Hamlet was a woman in disguise, which in turn gave critical warrant for Sarah Bernhardt to appear in the role. Freiligrath, the revolutionary poet, saw the fate of Germany symbolized in Hamlet's idealistic waverings. These, to Turgenev, seemed more characteristic of the Slavic temperament. Taine was more historically plausible, when he interpreted the characterization as a self-portrait of Shakespeare. But that would not serve to differentiate Hamlet from the playwright's other *dramatis personae*, all of them phases of himself, in a sense. It simply offered critics the opportunity to enlarge their personal repertories by playing Shakespeare as well as Hamlet.

Coleridge, whose public pronouncements did more than anything else to crystallize the notion of Shakespeare's hero as an impractical dreamer, goes on to comment revealingly in his

Table-Talk: 'I have a smack of Hamlet myself, if I may say so.' This candid aside is typically subjective; few readers would have dared to say as much; but most of them have responded in much the same way; and hence the multiplicity of their responses. The clearer-sighted Hazlitt formulated the principle involved, when he remarked: 'It is *we* who are Hamlet.' His formula is borne out by the fact that others have arrived at it independently, under widely differing circumstances: for example, the Russian critic Belinski or the French poet, Max Jacob. It was given an incisive restatement, several years ago, in the lecture-pamphlet of C. S. Lewis, *Hamlet: The Prince or the Poem.* It offers a simple and cogent explanation for the infinite variety of Hamlets, if we assume they have all been formed in that mirror of introspection which Shakespeare holds up to every individual. Hamlet has a smack of each of us, if we may say so. This is not to deny that he exists as a *persona* in his own right, with a strikingly high degree of individuality, so that we continue to argue and speculate about him as we do about other Shakespearean characters and—for that matter—other human beings. But his existence seems to reach out and touch ours, somewhat more intimately and more intensively than the kind of emotional involvement that the drama usually excites. It is rather more like those feelings of empathy which stimulate us, when we are reading a novel, to share the attitudes and relive the experiences of our favorite character.

Small wonder, then, if we cannot make up our minds about Hamlet's problems, or if we draw back from Horatio's task of reporting them aright. The conflicts of opinion they have aroused may never be reconciled; yet the controversy in itself is a powerful testimonial to the endlessly dynamic quality of the work; and we may, at least, agree that Hamlet means so many things to so many men because he invites them to put themselves in his place. If we begin with this conception of his character, we can safely proceed through it to the plot. That is the main thing, according to Aristotle, whose term for plot was the basis for our word *myth*. Here the distinctive feature seems to reside in a certain tension between the demands of the situation and the figure on whom they are made. Goethe may have overstressed the reluctant figure ('O cursed spite. . . !') and underemphasized the troublesome situation ('The time is out of joint.') However, he showed his usual sagacity in putting his finger on the line that sums up Hamlet's predicament; for Hamlet is, above all, a man in a plight, a mind resisting its body's destiny, a fighter against cosmic odds. This may be the case with all great tragic heroes, to some extent. If he stands out from the rest, it is partly because our identification with him seems more complete, but also because we are thereby enabled to face more directly the forces aligned against him. His position is a point of vantage from which we may look out with Shakespeare—and with the author whose reflective mood Shakespeare was dramatizing, Montaigne—upon 'this miserable human condition.' Hamlet is both the doubter and the doubt.

The central crux of the play, for some of its students, is not so much a schism in Hamlet's soul as a rift in Shakespeare's medium. T. S. Eliot, in his cavalier days, pronounced *Hamlet* 'most certainly an artistic failure,' on the grounds that it sought to communicate emotions which were in excess of the facts. Yet the facts are grim enough to constitute, for a recent existentialist writer, Jean Paris, 'the darkest story that any dramatist has ever conceived.' Since Mr. Eliot's topic was objectivity, he carefully avoided reading any emotions of his own into the text before him. 'No, I am not Prince Hamlet,' he could have said with J. Alfred Prufrock, 'nor was meant to be.' Abdicating, Mr. Eliot was thrown back upon the question-begging assumption that Shakespeare had some private purpose in view, which the intractable nature of his material kept him from satisfactorily expressing. Such an argument moves from the subjectivity of the romantics toward a more realistic scholarship, and toward the awareness of sources and conventions that has been accumulating meanwhile. To reconsider the tragedy in their light is to be impressed by its mixture of elements: its harsh outlines and rich surfaces, Gothic clowns and classical allusions, Viking prowess and humanistic learning, medieval superstition and modern skepticism, crude melodrama and subtle meditation. But we push the analysis too far, if it leaves us with nothing more than a tangle of improbabilities, beautifully embellished and imperfectly rationalized. However it may have been elaborated, *Hamlet* comprises for us an esthetic unity. The disparity between its primitive and its civilized components, which is an integral part of its fabric, is equally vital to its significance.

Once we have accepted this premise, our appreciation can only be enhanced by an understanding of the traditions to which Shakespeare's genius has given definitive form. The far-flung myths that converge in the tale of Hamlet have their fragmentary monument in Schick's *Corpus Hamleticum.* Mythographers, notably Gilbert Murray, would trace them to deeper and darker origins among seasonal rites. Freudianism, groping beneath the levels of consciousness, would perceive a similar pattern engraved upon the infant psyche. Such considerations can be relevant, if they help to account for responsive chords which are struck in us beyond the range of more purely critical perceptions. All the information we could muster would hardly suffice to elucidate the reasons why so unique a masterpiece has exerted so universal an appeal. And we are precluded from making any genetic study of *Hamlet* itself through the disappearance of its immediate source, the earlier play deducible from contemporaneous echoes—bywords for madness and revenge—which scholars have labeled with the pedantic but picturesque name of *Ur-Hamlet.* How much Shakespeare borrowed, how much he inherited, pending an unlikely discovery, we shall never know. Seek as we will, we are at a loss for counterparts. The Elizabethan repertory may suggest certain models: the atavistic genre of the Tragedy of Revenge, as inspired by Seneca and popularized by Kyd, undergoing the counter-influence of a more sophisticated development, the late innovation of Comical Satire as practiced by Ben Jonson and a newer school. But all these are subsumed in a larger design; and, even within the Shakespearean canon, *Hamlet* seems to occupy a special category.

Arnold Toynbee would arrange the plays, by the spiritual growth of their various heroes, in an ascending order which would correspond to the histories of civilizations. Hamlet would stand at the apogee because, with him, 'the field of action has been transferred from the Macrocosm to the Microcosm,' from man's outer to his inner world. The ascent from Hamlet's prototype in the Norse sagas to Shakespeare's humanist prince of the Renaissance would be a spectacular instance of what Mr. Toynbee calls 'etherealisation.' Kenneth Burke brings the cycle up to date by envisaging Hamlet as a scientist, a hint which may accord better with Shakespeare's intention than Hamlet as a nineteenth-century sentimentalist. At all events, we may fairly surmise that, when Shakespeare rewrote the *Ur-Hamlet*, he etherealized it. Its popularity was already assured, if only by its inherent blood and thunder; and Shakespeare, by mixing the comic with the tragic, was able to 'please all'—as one witness, Anthony Scoloker, tells us. But Shakespeare's *Hamlet* was likewise highly praised, by that intransigent intellectual, Gabriel Harvey, for its capacity 'to please the wiser sort.' The title page of the First Quarto goes out of its way to boast that the play was performed at both Oxford and Cambridge, though the text is too mutilated to justify the interest of a university audience. *Hamlet's* ultimate length, just under 4,000 lines, is one of the factors that give it exceptional status. *Macbeth*, which is no less exceptional for its shortness, is about half as long. But even if we omit both plays, in averaging the lengths of the others, we find a difference of more than a thousand lines between *Hamlet* and the median for Shakespeare's tragedies.

Thus the accepted version of *Hamlet*, based upon the Second Quarto and supplemented from the Folio, is by far the longest of Shakespeare's works—just as the title role is the longest of his parts, and practically the most extensive role in the annals of drama. What we can guess from the naïve First Quarto, with regard to actual performance, prompts us to wonder whether Shakespeare did not revise and augment and polish his script far beyond the normal usages of the playhouse. Could it have been presented uncut in his day, we may ask our stage-historians, or is that practice one of the rituals of a later Shakespearolatry? Coleridge was readier than we are to conclude that *Hamlet* had been intended for the study as well as the stage, that it had been addressed to the reader as well as the spectator. We would not willingly forgo the advantage, which we owe to a happy collaboration between those two interests, of viewing Shakespeare against the perspective of his theater. If Hamlet seems more interested in educational matters than any of Shakespeare's other protagonists, he is even more preoccupied with matters theatrical. Through the play-within-the-play and his colloquies with the Players, through frequent cross-reference and recurrent imagery, he loses no opportunity to display or discuss the conditions and standards of Shakespeare's craft. This, indeed, becomes one of the characteristics that set *Hamlet* apart as a piece of self-conscious craftsmanship. As it is dated, during the opening year or so of the seventeenth century, the closing years of Queen Elizabeth's reign, its composition marks a significant moment: Shakespeare's first attainment of full mastery and the beginning of his profoundest creative sequence.

The theater is always his main habitation; from it we depart at our own risk and to it we return for the most appropriate criteria. Yet whatever he has taken the pains to create deserves to be scanned and pondered at thoughtful leisure, and not less so when it deliberately exceeds his other creations in amplitude of scale, refinement of technique, and complexity of subject matter. That *Hamlet* is not a treatise on philosophy we may cheerfully admit, while recognizing that it abounds in philosophical implications and that many of these are explicitly underscored. Furthermore, the philosophers themselves could scarcely claim to have conclusively solved those metaphysical issues which Shakespeare has set forth dramatically. Living in the high Renaissance, he was able to retain his traditional contacts with the cultural inheritance, while becoming alert to intellectual currents which ultimately would sweep in our restless epoch. Galileo was his exact contemporary; well might Ophelia doubt that 'the sun doth move.' Shakespeare was also one of the first and most devoted readers of Montaigne in Florio's translation, as is evidenced by numerous turns of speech and by a certain essayistic movement of thought. This may be the tendency that Shaftesbury singled out in characterizing *Hamlet* as 'almost one continu'd *Moral*.' So it is, perforce, since the relationship of thought to action is an underlying theme, and since every action entails consideration of its consequences before and afterward. Hence the habit of generalization is strong, not merely in Hamlet but in all the others, from the sententious Polonius to the earthy Gravedigger. The style is charged with what the Germans term *geflügelte Worte*, those winged words which literature coins and men live by.

The very effectiveness of this diction has interposed a barrier between ourselves and the actions and thoughts of the play. It has been cited so often, for better and worse, that we are almost constrained to regard it as a contextual repository for favorite quotations and purple passages. We cannot—and would not—undo what Shakespeare has done to our language, though if we could we should hear his meanings more clearly. But we can make his statements abide our question, as Hamlet does the eloquence of Laertes:

> What is he whose grief
> Bears such an emphasis? whose phrase of sorrow
> Conjures the wand'ring stars, and makes them stand
> Like wonder-wounded hearers?
> (v.i.277–80)

The two words that establish the tone of this passage, 'emphasis' and 'phrase,' have been blurred for us by semantic erosion. Both were technical terms from the rhetorician's vocabulary. 'Phrase' meant roughly what it means to us; but it sounded artificial or pretentious; Bardolph does not understand it when Shallow uses it in *2 Henry IV* (III.ii.85). 'Emphasis,' which may sound common and colorless, would have been an unexpected word, rather self-consciously designating violence of expression. Hamlet is understandably obsessed by the varying degrees of correspondence between emotions and words. Previously, he has checked himself from expressing his sorrow in public. Now, when Laertes emerges as chief mourner for Ophelia, Hamlet betrays his own grief by challenging the sincerity of Laertes. The latter, standing in the grave, has just delivered himself of a grandiose tirade in the Senecan manner. Hamlet, in half a minute, will emulate him by leaping in, announcing his identity, and ranting even more melodramatically. Poised at the brink in the mean while, he criticizes his rival, echoing and outdoing Laertes' phraseology as he calls the cosmos to witness. Laertes and—by implication—Hamlet are actors playing to an audience of wandering stars; and these are presumably smitten by wonder, the spectatorial reaction that Horatio bespeaks at the outset and at the conclusion. One of Hamlet's questions leads to another: whether the stagecraft lives up to the situation? and who should its spokesman be, if not Hamlet himself?

Shakespeare's consciousness of how such effects were obtained should be our frame of reference in seeking to understand them. Since drama—more than any other form of literature—depends upon a peculiar set of material conditions, we try as we reread the play to restage it in the mind's eye, drawing upon what we have learned or conjectured about Elizabethan dramatic production. Since plays can be vehicles for ideas, as this play has so spectacularly been, we can illuminate it by our recourse to the history of ideas. But since it is, primarily and finally, a verbal structure, our scrutiny is most concretely rewarded at the level of phrase and emphasis. As a poet, thinking in images which he phrases for vocal projection, Shakespeare addresses our minds through our eyes and ears. Moving line-by-line from scene to scene, yet glancing backward and forward occasionally, we may notice how the temporal flow of his verse is regulated by formal rhythms and organized by thematic continuities. His principles of composition are not enunciated in manifestoes or prefaces; yet they are always close at hand, if we remember how thoroughly he was schooled in rhetoric and how consciously he handled its devices. Nor should we forget that its sister arts were grammar and logic, if we would see in his own terms how his words cohere and his thoughts develop. The linguistic discipline of the Trivium, which Hamlet might still have encountered at Wittenberg, may well renew its relevance today, when criticism is manifestly looking for more analytical methods. The danger might be, as it has been in the past, that means are frequently mistaken for ends. But in this case, where the impact has been so great that it has deflected attention from the work itself, that is the least of the risks we shall be taking.

THE QUESTION OF HAMLET

I. INTERROGATION

THe sentiment of Alexandre Dumas, that 'Shakespeare is the poet who created most after God,' carries us well to the other side of idolatry. If we share it, it is our best warrant for the idea of the artist as a creator and of his art as a world in miniature. Shakespeare himself, from what little we know about him, would have been much embarrassed by the analogy; his wry impulse, when he talks about poets, is to compare them with lunatics, lovers, and liars. On the other hand, conceiving his function in the downright terms of craftsmanship, he also conceived of God as a master craftsman, the Ultimate Playwright, 'your only jig-maker'—an impious ejaculation which also implies that life is a farce (III.ii.132). Hamlet is interrupted by Rosencrantz's announcement of the Players; and the comparison is reinforced with a digression on the public actors, 'the tragedians of the city' now traveling in such foreign parts as Denmark, and their juvenile rivals, 'that cry out on the top of question' and 'exclaim against their own succession' (II.ii.342, 354–5, 368). As for bad acting, it prompts the unhappy thought that the race of men must have been created by some bungling demiurge in the cosmic workshop, by 'Nature's journeymen'; for the Master Craftsman could have had no part in fashioning such abominable imitations of humanity (III.ii.33–4). Man, the authentic masterpiece of God and Nature, is significantly described as 'a piece of work'—an expression which Hamlet goes on to use twice more in describing the play-within-the-play (51, 250). If that play, 'The Murder of Gonzago,' is Hamlet's exposure of the old King's death, then the encompassing drama of *Hamlet* itself may be viewed as Shakespeare's attempt to probe even more deeply into occulted matters.

When Hamlet cudgels his brains by putting his hands to his head and speaking of 'this distracted globe,' he is positing a relationship between the microcosm of man's intelligence and the macrocosm, the outer world (I.v.97.) He may likewise have been suggesting—to those ears which were first attuned to his words—how that disproportionate relationship might find a connecting link through the theatrical medium, and through a particular theater known as the Globe. At this point, during Hamlet's Second Soliloquy, he proceeds to write upon his tables. The business is characteristic; for, in the course of the play, he is called upon to do a good deal of writing. One of his poems is exhibited; three of his letters are communicated; and we hear of still others, one of which does him yeoman's service in his most dangerous emergency. His most important gesture, as a writer, is to set down a speech for interpolation in 'The Murder of Gonzago'; and he is so exhilarated by the success of the performance that he entertains the fancy of turning professional, of acquiring a share—like Shakespeare himself—in a company of actors. 'Half a share,' Horatio dryly banters; after all, the Players deserve some credit for the collaboration (III.ii.290). Claudius, with mounting suspicion, has asked for the name of the play; and Hamlet has answered, 'The Mousetrap.' That is his private joke, since he has devised the stratagem in order to catch the conscience of the King. But the young scholar, instead of explaining, taunts and tantalizes the royal spectator: 'Marry, how? Tropically' (247). A listener who heard no more than Claudius would comprehend no more than a tautological pun, which is spelled out by the Quarto reading, 'Trapically.'

The basic meaning, encapsulated in Hamlet's pedantic term, affords a clue to the trick he is playing on Claudius. Moreover, it offers a hint for interpreting Shakespeare's dramatic method. The trap is a trope, a twist of phrasing, a figurative means of expressing the play's intended effect. Insofar as words may be transferred from one context to another, insofar as carefully chosen symbols must be substituted for more casual and confused actualities, all drama, indeed all literary representation, depends on the use of tropes. Control over them is like the power of Prospero, whose magic is the 'tropical' expression of Shakespeare's stagecraft. The official discipline for the attainment of such mastery was, in his day, the art of rhetoric. Shakespeare displays his conversance with that art even when he is satirizing it, as in *Love's Labour's Lost*. No mere enumeration of verbal schemes could show how he was able to animate them; and no two rhetoricians would quite agree on categories and terminologies; hence their theory cannot entirely be trusted as a guide to his practice. However, there are certain formal concepts which correspond to dominant moods in his work. 'Hamlet's world,' Maynard Mack has lately noted, 'is pre-eminently in the interrogative mood.' Precisely; and this questioning spirit takes a structural form which invites a technical analysis. The interchange of question and answer, as a basis of dialogue, is fundamental to dramatic technique; and dialogue, whenever it serves a purpose, becomes dialectic. In the stichomythy of Greek tragedy, it serves not only to forward the exposition but to precipitate the discovery. Shakespeare is adroit in his handling of it throughout his work: note how he opens the first four scenes of *Macbeth*, or brings out the inquisitorial predisposition of King Lear. Comparative statistics would prove little, given the variances of Elizabethan punctuation; but Hamlet's Graveyard Scene provides a cogent sampling, with seventy question-marks in 322 lines.

What is more revealing, the word 'question' occurs in *Hamlet* no less than seventeen times, much more frequently than in any of Shakespeare's other plays. Recalling that it comes as the final word in Hamlet's most famous line, we may well regard it as the key-word of the play. Many other words contribute to the general atmosphere of uncertainty, as we shall soon have occasion to recall. Furthermore, besides direct inquiry, there are other modes of questioning, notably doubt and irony, which we shall be considering in due sequence. Each of these three devices is a figure of speech and simultaneously a figure of thought, to take them as they are categorized by Quintilian. This overlapping classification is useful, if it helps us to understand how words adapt their structure to ideas, how the very process of cogitation can be dramatized. *Interrogatio* is the simplest mode, with the rhetorical question indicating its own response, or with the catechism preordaining its set replies. But when the answer is unforeseen, or when there is no answer—that is the kind of open question which *Hamlet* is more particularly concerned to pose. The play begins with such a question: 'Who's there?' This, at first glance, would seem to be no more than a sentry's perfunctory challenge. With the second line and its counter-question, we become aware that the original speaker was not the sentry on duty but the nervous officer who has just arrived to relieve him. As the exposition develops, we come to realize that the change of guard constitutes a symbolic prologue, a re-enactment of those dynastic changes which frame the play. *Qui vive? Vive le roi!* The watchword, in ghostly reverberation, gathers ironic overtones. 'Long live the King!' Which king? *Le roi est mort. Vive le roi!*

Now Bernardo, the arriving sentry, presumably knew that Francisco, the watchman, was there. Whom else then, we may wonder, could he have been expecting to encounter? 'Who's there?' might be the cry of a frightened child in the dark; it might also be the query of a metaphysician scanning the void for evidence of God. The nocturnal setting from which it is launched, a fortified elevation by the edge of a northern sea, an outpost of reason on the frontier of unconsciousness, starkly accords with the interrogative theme. Francisco's departure strikes the note of foreboding: the night is very cold and he is heartsick. The entrance of Horatio and Marcellus, with their expository conversation, raises further questions: why are these feverish preparations for war going on in the background, nightly as well as daily? and can this be some civic portent, which we are here to watch, like the baneful omens that portended the fall of Caesar at Rome? Speculations are rife during the interim of suspense between the appearance and the reappearance of the Ghost, which is nothing if not a personified question. 'This thing...' Marcellus calls it, 'this dreaded sight..., this apparition' (I.i.21, 25, 28). The phrase 'like the King' occurs four times, twice in a question and twice in an assertion (41, 43, 58, 110). As a scholar, versed in such arcane investigations, Horatio has been urged to 'question it.' The wraith, perhaps offended, has not replied to his interrogation: 'What art thou that usurp'st this time of night... ?' (46). The same verb will fall with greater impact upon the usurping Claudius, in the last spoken line of the play-within-the-play: '...On wholesome life usurp immediately' (III.ii.271). Horatio's next effort to interrogate the Ghost is a more explicit conjuration. It allows for various explanations as to the nature and possible intent of the phenomenon; but again it evokes no answering whisper out of the darkness.

In the following scene, the brilliantly lighted Council Scene, it is Hamlet who is questioned in turn by Claudius and Gertrude. His answers are reluctant and elusive, preceded by an enigmatic aside and followed by his First Soliloquy, which voices his melancholy state of mind and especially his distaste for his mother's remarriage. After this self-questioning, Horatio and Marcellus arrive to tell him about the Ghost, and he responds with a volley of questions to them: 'Saw? who?... But where was this?... Did you not speak to it?... Arm'd, say you?... Stay'd it long?... His beard was grizzled–no?' (I.ii.190–240). Subsequently he has his turn as investigator; and he too is overwhelmingly conscious of the conflicting possibilities that might account for this 'questionable shape.' Why has the tomb cast up a corpse, if indeed it has? What can it mean, and what can it lead to? 'Say, why is this? wherefore? what should we do?' (I.iv.57). The spectre will not speak until Hamlet faces it alone, ignoring the terrors envisioned by Horatio. Horatio, as befits a student from Wittenberg University, has been skeptical; he has begun by saying 'tush' and attributing the manifestation to fantasy; but he has come around to believing, at least 'in part.' The Ghost's narration, with its pointed refusal to reveal the purgatorial secrets of its prison house, ends by deepening the mystery. Hamlet's reaction to the disclosure of his father's murder and his uncle's hypocrisy is registered in his Second Soliloquy. His new awareness, that Claudius could smile and be a villain, makes him distrustful of everyone about him. Hesitant to impart what the Ghost has confided, he swears his companions to a conspiratorial secrecy, while the Ghost's voice echoes from the cellarage, the cavernous area under the Elizabethan stage that was commonly designated as hell.

Hamlet is understandably anxious to identify this ambiguous figure with the late King, his father, and consequently to trust it. But Horatio's doubt cannot be dismissed so easily. It is already present as an alternative at the moment of recognition:

> Be thou a spirit of health or goblin damn'd,
> Bring with thee airs from heaven or blasts from hell...
> (I.iv.40–41)

And from that moment Hamlet is constantly glancing upward and downward, balancing every decision and making every move in full view of a perspective which now extends, as in the medieval mysteries, from the celestial to the infernal sphere. 'Heaven and earth!' was his exclamation in the First Soliloquy (I.ii.142). The Second widens his frame of reference:

> O all you host of heaven! O earth! What else?
> And shall I couple hell? (I.v.92–3)

Whether heaven or hell is ordinant, whether good or evil prevails in this world, seems to hinge on Hamlet's identification of the Ghost. Yet that would not resolve the ambiguity; for if he takes the Ghost's word, the world is far more corrupt than he has previously imagined; but if the Ghost is false, then that corruption undermines the very foundations of the universe. Taking our ghostly witness at face value, we might recognize it as the soul of Hamlet the Elder, returning to earth on a special mission from purgatory, in accordance with the orthodox tenets of the Catholic faith. The Reformation, however, rejected the dogma of purgatory; and we associate Wittenberg with Protestantism. The ardent Protestant soon to be King of England had recently published a treatise arguing that ghosts were not souls of the dead but demons who tempted the living. Whether Hamlet was being led astray to eternal damnation or being enjoined to perform a sacred duty would thus be contingent on theological questions which were moot. Even more perplexing are the moral implications of the Ghost's command. It is based upon the *lex talionis*, the primitive law of the blood-feud, whereby the nearest of kin to a murdered person is bound to avenge him by slaying his murderer. This barbarous principle, which Hamlet seems ready to act on, runs counter to both the Catholic and Protestant religions. It is altogether incompatible with the teachings of Christianity. 'Vengeance is mine,' says the Lord, in both the Old and New Testaments, 'I will repay.'

Hamlet's outlook is clouded by two problematic assumptions, closely related yet somewhat contradictory, each of them deeply rooted in tradition yet increasingly subject to questioning: the belief in ghosts and the code of revenge. Happily, it is not for us to solve his problems; it is enough if we appreciate their immediacy to him and their complexity for him. Leaving our questioner momentarily to his double dilemma, we shift our ground to a simpler norm and a lower degree of tension, as Shakespeare often does for dramatic relief. This can be exemplified by Laertes, who is destined to be Hamlet's foil and to call his own father's death 'in question' (IV.V.217). He is contrasted with Hamlet from their introductory scene, when the King grants him leave to return to Paris while insisting that Hamlet remain at Elsinore. The difference between his liberty as a private individual and Hamlet's public responsibility as a prince is emphasized by Laertes' farewell to Ophelia; his emphasis on the word 'safety' brings out a difference between the perilous outworks and the secure interiors of the castle, between the witching time of night and the reassurance of the morning air (I.iii.21, 43). The domestic underplot seems to promise a pleasant relaxation from the dynastic plot. Instead of the strained relations between nephew-stepson, uncle-stepfather, and widow-mother-wife, we are introduced to the family circle of brother-son, sister-daughter, and father. First brother advises sister; then father advises son; and finally daughter is advised by father. By this time suspicion has operated to entrammel the underplot with the main plot. 'Happy families are all alike,' as Tolstoy has observed. 'Every unhappy family is unhappy in its own way.'

The character of Polonius has been treated with much greater respect by the commentators than it is by Hamlet himself.

We might even infer, in the case of Dr. Johnson, a sense of personal affinity. Shakespeare's problem, in characterizing the elderly counsellor, was to portray a bore without becoming one —a problem which defeated Pope in *The Dunciad*. Shakespeare solved it by endowing Polonius with some traits of the *senex* in classical comedy, the heavy father who amuses us by boring himself along with his interlocutor: 'What was I about to say?' (II.i.49–50). He is the exponent in this play of the perennial conflict between crabbed age and flaming youth. We, the audience, unlike the commentators, side with youth, suppressing a yawn when sententiousness is underlined by 'Mark you' or 'Perpend.' We put up with age's pomposity and prolixity because we suspect that his admonitions will go unheeded and that he himself is headed for disaster. In the mean while he holds forth with his set-piece, which has found its appropriate immortality by being charactered in the memories of generations of schoolboys. Many contemporary parallels for it have been adduced, but only to establish the fact that such precepts were the commonplaces of copybook humanism. Seriously and dramatically, they enunciate the standards of conduct that Hamlet has just accepted by agreeing to stay on as the 'chiefest courtier' and heir presumptive of Claudius. Those courtly and political values are largely negative. 'Give thy thoughts no tongue'—first and foremost, Laertes, never speak your mind. 'Nor any unproportion'd thought his act'—and never do anything, Hamlet, without first thinking it out (I.iii. 59, 60). That is acting, in more ways than one; how to act at court has it analogies with how to act on the stage; and the advice of Polonius to Laertes will have its parody in the advice of Hamlet to the Players.

What not to say, what to wear, how to take care of one's money, how to make a good impression on others—it is all very sane and sensible, all very practical and prudent behavior. But it is etiquette rather than ethics; it is rather the worldly wisdom of Bacon than the self-searching of Montaigne. Or so it would seem until the final maxim, which comes as a magnificent *non sequitur:*

> This above all—to thine own self be true,
> And it must follow, as the night the day,
> Thou canst not then be false to any man. (78–80)

Up to this point the counsel is 'other-directed,' to apply the convenient term of a modern sociologist; yet the concluding precept is 'inner-directed.' Therefore it will be worthier of Hamlet, who cuts through a tangle of insincerities, than of Laertes, who 'recks not his own rede' (51). The two scenes that follow, 'as the night the day,' in the succession of nights and days that accelerate the dramatic rhythm, contrast the mundane picture of father and son with the otherworldly interview between Hamlet and the Ghost. Hamlet's comments while waiting, on how a 'particular fault' may impair a person's or country's honor, have been wrested from their context to demonstrate that Shakespeare was an Aristotelian, and that he made Hamlet allude to his own tragic flaw (I.iv.36). Primarily, they refer to Claudius, and to the bad reputation his bibulous habits are gaining for Denmark. Inferentially, they comment upon Polonius, whom we overhear shortly afterward, ordering Reynaldo to lay 'slight sullies' on the repute of Laertes abroad (II.i.39). The servant is ordered to spy upon the son, to find out what other Danes may be in Paris, 'And how, and who, what means, and where they keep' (8). Then, in the course of conversation or 'drift of question,' Reynaldo is to play the *agent provocateur*. He is to circulate mildly scandalous rumors about Laertes, in the hope that these will elicit gossip of genuine scandals.

It is ironic to hark back, in this connection, to the initial exchange between brother and sister, when young Laertes—truly the son of his father—solemnly warned Ophelia against youthful indiscretions. Her reply was to warn him, with gentle irony, against talking like a Pharisee and behaving like a libertine. Now Polonius, through his eagerness to see his own son implicated in misbehavior, betrays a distrustful and cynical attitude toward human nature underneath his thin mask of concern for the world's good opinion. His discussion of Hamlet's love, with Ophelia, has been tainted by the same low-mindedness. It is curious that a marriage between this couple should be considered out of the question by both Polonius and Laertes—who will himself be pushed forward as a candidate for the throne. It is clear, from the Queen's later remarks, that she would have welcomed the match; but Gertrude is, of course, in no position to be critical of other people's marriages. Hamlet's monologues are characteristically devoted to the most rigorous self-examination: 'Am I a coward? / Who calls me villain?' (II.ii.598–9). Polonius realizes his talents most fully by delivering himself of a lengthy oration, which keeps harping on the rhetorical question: 'What might you think?' (129, 134–5, 139). The answer is not so obvious as he would indignantly suppose. Claudius and Gertrude might very plausibly think that he was willing to look the other way while Ophelia flirted with Hamlet, since Polonius is just about to propose that she be utilized as a decoy while he and the King spy upon her and Hamlet from behind an arras. His instructions to Reynaldo have laid down the pattern for an elaborate game of espionage and counter-espionage. 'Your bait of falsehood takes this carp of truth' (II.i.63).

Accordingly, when Polonius tries to sound Hamlet, 'Do you know me. . . ?,' Hamlet's responsive epithet, 'You are a fishmonger,' is not completely far-fetched (II.ii.173, 174). Elizabethan ribaldry sometimes neutralized the Lenten distinction between dealers in fish and dealers in flesh. Fish will be associated with worms, and worms with corpses, in Hamlet's later reflections upon the biological cycle (IV.iii.27–30). Behind the fishmonger Polonius, he will have discerned the fisherman Claudius, who will have 'Thrown out his angle for my proper life' (V.ii.66). For the moment, when Polonius disclaims the epithet, he gives Hamlet the opportunity to retort: 'Then I would you were so honest a man' (II.ii.176). Honesty has become an obsession with him, since the revelation of the Ghost. If 'it is an honest ghost,' then those human beings to whom Hamlet stood closest have behaved dishonestly (I.v.138). They have been false to him, in being untrue to themselves. We must reconsider, one by one, the identity of all the others; and, since he himself has been behaving strangely, they must take their turns examining him. The play comprises a series of colloquies in which, like the sentries challenging one another, the characters successively ask: 'Who's there?' The question, 'Are you honest?,' acquires a poignant inflection when it is addressed to Ophelia; for the adjective, as applied to a woman, means chaste (III.i.103). Hamlet professes himself 'indifferent honest,' tolerably honest, that is to say; but all men are sinners, and women too, knaves and harlots (123). If the virginal Ophelia is to be exempt from the common destiny, she must not walk in the sun; she must not stay at the court. The only place for her is a nunnery.

Hamlet is torn between a lover's desire to believe in her and a distrust of her as Polonius' daughter. His suspicions seem to be confirmed; apparently he catches sight of Polonius, obtruding his inquisitive head from the arras; and the dialogue shifts, accordingly, from blank verse to distracted prose. 'I did love you once,' he tells her (115–16). Then, suspecting collusion, he takes back the declaration, even as she has given back his presents: 'I loved you not' (119–20). In her rejoinder, 'I was the more deceived,' Mrs. Siddons is said to have concentrated the essence of the role. If Hamlet did not love Ophelia, she has indeed been deceived; but since he did, and probably still does, she is deceived all the more by his denial; and he completes his multiple deception by convincing her that he has gone mad. Yet he too is deceived, if he thinks of her as a party to the intrigue against him; she is merely an unwitting accomplice, who is not told about the eavesdropping until afterward; hence she is also a victim of her father's deceit. Polonius continues to 'hunt . . . the trail of policy' (II.ii.47); but his fishing expedition, baited though the angle was with Ophelia, has failed to take the carp of truth; the elder statesman must try another ruse. Meanwhile the King and Queen have attempted to sound the Prince through their own emissaries, a pair of his former schoolmates. Rosencrantz and Guildenstern are not really bad fellows; the trouble with them is that they are professional good fellows; their character is to have no character. Their backstage nicknames are the Knife and Fork, partly because they are inseparable, and partly because it is their task to feed Hamlet his lines.

In Rosencrantz and Guildenstern, as in Ophelia, Hamlet is strongly drawn to repose his confidence. But with them the ties of early friendship, as he gradually realizes, have been strained and twisted by the ways of the court. On their side, as it is later reported to the Queen and the King, they find him

> Niggard of question, but of our demands
> Most free in his reply. (III.i.13–14)

Actually, he does most of the talking and asks most of the questions, deftly turning their proposed inquiry into a cross-examination. It starts as the amiable repartee of schoolfellows, meeting again after a number of years and recounting how fortune has treated them. But honesty is always the main issue between Hamlet and his interlocutors; and here it is interjected by Rosencrantz, with his news 'that the world's grown honest' (II.ii.241). News indeed; and Hamlet caps the sardonic jest with the conclusion that doomsday must be at hand. 'Let me question more in particular,' he persists (243). But they do not converse about the outside world; rather, he dwells upon Denmark—or rather, upon his sense of confinement within it. This seems to strengthen their unspoken hypothesis, that he is suffering from disappointment at not having succeeded to the throne. When he complains of 'bad dreams,' obliquely referring to the visitation of the Ghost, it is Guildenstern who presumes to offer a piece of unworldly wisdom: 'the very substance of the ambitious is merely the shadow of a dream' (265). Hamlet, whose discrimination between shadows and substances is somewhat more acute than theirs, embroiders the paradox. Suddenly he appeals to them, by the rights of fellowship, the claims of shared adolescence: 'Were you not sent for? Is it your own inclining?' (282). Their embarrassment is a full confession. They have yielded to his scrutiny; he is still inscrutable to them.

His appeal is to their latent sincerity: 'be even and direct with me' (299). But the court is the realm of Machiavellian policy, where falsehood is the habitual instrument, and where the devious modes of procedure are set by the Chamberlain, who boasts of using 'indirections' to 'find directions out' (II.i.66). Hamlet, confronted at the outset by mystery, has resorted to mystification. He has—as he promised Horatio and Marcellus—'put an antic disposition on' (I.v.172). He has assumed a clownish pose, a manner of speaking by obscure fits and outspoken starts, a role which conceals his intentions by inviting all sorts of bewildered conjecture. 'Madness in great ones must not unwatch'd go' (III.i.196). It seems to be the consensus among his observers that he is mad; but observations vary according to point of view. Polonius attributes the derangement to frustrated love; Rosencrantz and Guildenstern ascribe it to frustrated ambition; and there is something in both of these diagnoses. Had his father died a normal death, had his mother observed a respectable widowhood, Hamlet might well have attained the crown and married Ophelia. But such frustrations are attendant upon that two-sided burden of anxieties which he must carry alone: the Ghost, the revenge. Claudius, disturbed by the transformation, can see no reason for it 'More than his father's death' (II.ii.8). Gertrude, slightly more sensitive to her son's reactions, senses a further vexation: 'His father's death and our o'erhasty marriage' (58). This is exactly where Hamlet himself stands, in his opening scene. At that stage he would be satisfied, if not happy, simply to leave the prison of Denmark and lead a scholar's life at Wittenberg.

At the stage where Rosencrantz and Guildenstern confront him, he has much more on his mind than he can unburden to them. But since they have been direct enough to admit their royal errand, Hamlet is co-operative enough to render a diagnosis of his melancholia. Avoiding any specific motivation, he generalizes upon his own disquietude until he seems to be diagnosing the malady of an age—and, more than that, the *taedium vitae*, the *Weltschmerz*, the *ennui* of every sentient mind in mid-career, pausing to ask whether life itself has a meaning or a direction. Embedded in Hamlet's elegiac discourse, which sustains the world-weary tone of his first soliloquy, is his paean to the greatness of humanity: 'What a piece of work is a man!' Since the text of this passage has been subjected to considerable argument, it is worth noticing that the Folio punctuates the subsequent clauses with question-marks rather than exclamation-points: 'how noble in reason? how infinite in faculties? in form and moving how express and admirable? in action how like an angel? in apprehension how like a god?' (II.ii.313–16). Hamlet's mood, at all events, is interrogative rather than exclamatory. And it is at this timely conjunction that, with the arrival of the Players, fortune drops a means of interrogation into his hands. His greeting to them is Shakespeare's salute to his craft; and their demonstration of it, the Player's Speech, conjures up two suppressed images of passion, a murdered king and a mourning queen. 'What's Hecuba to him, or he to Hecuba. . .?' (585). If a mere actor can feel a part in which he has no emotional involvement, what of a wife whose husband has been assassinated? Or a son who is pledged to revenge the assassination? Or the assassin–how would he react to a reconstruction of the crime? Hamlet's Third Soliloquy, terminating the Second Act, sets the stage for the play-within-the-play.

Two separate lines of questioning have converged in failure: that of Claudius and Gertrude, with Rosencrantz and Guildenstern as their intermediaries, and that of Polonius, both in person and through the person of Ophelia. It is high time for Hamlet to take the offensive and test the Ghost's accusations. Old Truepenny is also on trial, since it is a question of his illusory word against the smiling actuality of Claudius. 'He that plays the king shall be welcome–' so Hamlet has greeted the Players, adding with a grim nuance, 'his Majesty shall have tribute of me' (II.ii.332–3). Hamlet has his tables to remind him of what he is quite unlikely to forget, that Claudius himself is no less accomplished an actor than the Play-King. We have come a long way from the innocent young man of two months ago, whose feelings of grief were so directly externalized by his garments of mourning that he could exclude the verb *seems* from his personal vocabulary. 'Seems, madam? Nay, it is.' (I.ii.76). This grammatical distinction has been sublimated into a metaphysical abstraction, by André Gide in his French translation: '*Apparence? Ah! Non! Madame. Réalité.*' It is the unavoidable jingle of the German metaphysicians, *schein* and *sein*. Hamlet begins to repudiate the abstraction, to recognize that an apparent reality can be a deceptive appearance, when the paternal apparition denounces his 'seeming-virtuous queen' (I.v.46). Now, when Hamlet is setting his mousetrap for the detection of Claudius, he stations Horatio to keep his eye on the King. For once a spy will report back to Hamlet, and not to his mighty opposite. After the play—and no interruption seems to be anticipated—Hamlet and Horatio will compare notes upon the demeanor of Claudius, 'In censure of his seeming' (III.ii.92).

But Claudius still has an eye upon Hamlet, and is attending the play to humor him. Though a less suspicious nature than the King's might smell a rat in the dumb-show, he does not react verbally until after the cloying dialogue between the Play-King and the Play-Queen. Then, uneasily, he inquires of Hamlet: 'Have you heard the argument? Is there no offence in't?' Hamlet is as good as a chorus, an officious impresario who underscores the performance by hissing a commentary, addressing bitter ironies to Gertrude and outrageous ribaldries to Ophelia, 'metal more attractive' (III.ii.116). To Claudius his polite disclaimer is a covert indictment: 'No, no! They do but jest; poison in jest; no offence i'th'world' (III.ii.244–5). Everybody loves a good joke; this will amuse you. The same wordplay ensued, after his colloquy with the Ghost, when Hamlet apologized for having possibly offended Horatio. Horatio returned the politeness with 'no offence.' Whereupon Hamlet, his mind on the crime, insisted that there was: 'And much offence too' (I.v.135–7). The offence of Claudius, brought to the surface by 'The Murder of Gonzago,' becomes the thrice-reiterated theme of the King's remorseful soliloquy in the following scene: 'O my offence is rank, it smells to heaven' (III.iii.36). Examining the case of his own conscience, he proves to be just as shrewd and relentless at catechizing himself as he is at manipulating others. He cannot purge his soul of guilt without repenting, and he cannot repent while still enjoying the spoils of murder. 'May one be pardon'd and retain th'offence?' (56). Clearly not; but, though Claudius is enough of a theologian to apprehend the consequences, he is too hardened a sinner to relinquish his queen or crown. His conscience is caught:

> O limed soul, that struggling to be free,
> Art more engag'd! (68–9)

Hamlet's Sixth Soliloquy follows hard upon this unique soliloquy of Claudius. Now that the Ghost's word has been verified, Hamlet can hasten to consummate his vendetta. Before that he must heed the summons of his mother; and in his brief, impatient Fifth Soliloquy, he has resolved to be stern with her; but before he can be, as it happens, he chances on Claudius at his prayers. It is the opportune moment. Or is it? That is the question. 'That would be scann'd' (III.iii.75). It is uncharacteristic of Claudius to be concerning himself with his salvation. The late King Hamlet, though he was less of a sensualist than his brother, is probably suffering in purgatory because he died without the last rites of the Church, 'unhous'led' and 'unanel'd' (I.v.77). The only way to get even with Claudius is, quite literally, to see him damned. Therefore Hamlet delays, awaiting some more sinful moment, when Claudius' death will mean his certain damnation. This delay has become the *vexata quaestio* of critical interpretations. Dr. Johnson was utterly horrified by the speech, as anyone must be who accepts its eschatological premises; he saw that the Christian conception of the afterlife was being exploited to further a monstrously un-Christian trespass. Other critics, less capable of taking the next world so literally, have traced Hamlet's scruples to a humane recoil or even a sentimental vacillation, rather than to a terrible resolve. Others have argued that his casuistry was a pretext for self-deception which hid motives discernible only to psychoanalysis; or that Shakespeare has somehow failed to adjust the situation to his hero's—or his own—emotions; or else that tradition had imposed upon him an anachronistic set of crude materials, which could be endlessly embellished but never integrated.

For all these criticisms, on varying levels, the common stumbling block is the code of revenge, the cult of blood for blood, the incongruity of a civilized man carrying out so barbaric an imperative, flouting the laws of God and man by taking his enemy's punishment into his own hands. But Hamlet, though he repines against his plight in general, never questions his duty of killing the King. On the other hand, he never deliberately acts upon it; here, where he considers it most punctiliously, he concludes in favor of temporary inaction; and when he acts at the end, it is in spontaneous retaliation for several other deaths—including, in a minute or two, his own. To be sure, he moves with too much haste in the Closet Scene; and the result is disastrous enough to warrant his previous hesitation; for the slaying of Polonius alerts the King to Hamlet's intentions toward himself, and enables him to regain the initiative. Polonius might well have taken Hamlet's brutal pun as a caveat, after he boasted of having performed the leading role in a college play about Julius Caesar (III.ii.108–11). Spying and prying for the last time from his favorite vantage-point behind the arras, the busybody can rise to ironic prophecy: 'I'll silence me even here' (III.iv.4). Before he ceases to be a spectator, he witnesses at least the confrontation between Hamlet and the Queen. Again the theme is offence, as the mother accuses the son of offending his father's memory. 'Come, come, you answer with an idle tongue,' she reprimands him. Stichomythy adds to the sharpness of his line, as he reverses her reprimand: 'Go, go, you question with a wicked tongue' (11–12).

With the silencing of Polonius, his plan for Gertrude to chide Hamlet is dropped; thereafter it is Hamlet who chides Gertrude. 'Have you eyes?' he demands, and repeats his rhetorical question (65, 67). How, then, could she have shown such insensibility?

> Eyes without feeling, feeling without sight,
> Ears without hands or eyes, smelling sans all . . . (78–9)

'. . .Sans everything' was, pertinently enough, the terminal phrase of Jaques' speech about the ages of man. This utter negation of all the senses stirs Hamlet to a denunciation of sensuality. Youth denouncing age for carnal indulgence, the child reproving the parent, that reversal of roles is unnatural, as he is all too painfully aware. Unexpectedly, as if to test Gertrude's perceptions, or to show up her husband's carnality against his predecessor's spirituality, the Ghost appears; and his untimely visit interrupts the meeting of minds between mother and son. 'Do you see nothing there?' cries Hamlet. 'Nor did you nothing hear?' (131,133). Gertrude is nonplussed; and, inasmuch as the Ghost remains invisible to her, it is easy for her to reduce it to a hallucination, the subjective consequence of Hamlet's madness or 'ecstasy.' For an uncertain interval, it is hard to say who is investigating whom, or on what spiritual or material plane. The Ghost's last exit, like its first entrance, is hedged with unanswered questions; but, unlike the mute shade of Banquo, it leaves behind an oral message. Its old injunction is urgently renewed; and that renewal, coming so quickly after the Prayer Scene, suggests that the Ghost is much less troubled by theological niceties than Hamlet. It tempts us to revert to Hamlet's original dubiety: was this really a Christian soul? or was it a pagan spirit? or could it have been the devil after all, leading Hamlet on to damn himself?

The death of Polonius is on his head, in any case, and he is on the defensive once again. He can hide the body, insult his enemies openly, and challenge them to catch him, as if the whole thing were a children's game: 'Hide fox, and all after!' (IV.ii.31). But the jig is up; and as he leaves for England, escorted by Rosencrantz and Guildenstern with secret orders for his execution, it would seem that he had abysmally failed.

Briefly we glimpse him at the Danish border, interrogating a captain who explains why the Norwegian army is crossing it from the other direction. It will take more than two thousand lives to fight out the sovereignty of this barren strip of Polish borderland, to 'debate the question of this straw' (IV.iv.26). Yet, as Hamlet soliloquizes in his last and most decisive meditation, true greatness would 'find quarrel in a straw' when honor is at stake. (55) 'The question of these wars,' personified by the Ghost, has been in the air from the start (I.i.111). Horatio's exposition, the embassy of Voltemand and Cornelius, the other reports and allusions have kept us in touch with the relations between the ruling houses of Denmark and Norway. The King of Norway's nephew, Fortinbras, is Hamlet's counterpart on the public level of the overplot, just as Laertes is on the private level of the underplot. Fortinbras, with his victorious army, has been avenging King Hamlet's defeat of his father, King Fortinbras, just as Laertes will seek to be revenged 'Most throughly' for his father, Polonius (IV.v.136). And, just as Fortinbras sets an example for Hamlet, so Hamlet sympathetically perceives that his own situation has its parallel in that of Laertes:

> For by the image of my cause I see
> The portraiture of his. (V.ii.77–8)

But the contrast is still more striking than the comparison; for the rash Laertes, goaded on by Claudius, feels none of Hamlet's compunctions. Rather than spare a praying enemy, Laertes would be perfectly willing 'To cut his throat i'th' church!' (IV.vii.127). And Claudius would concur: 'Revenge should have no bounds.' Laertes' re-entrance, at the head of an angry mob, brings to a climax those rumblings of political discontent which, along with threats of foreign invasion, have been jeopardizing the state of Denmark. That disorder of the body politic coincides with the distraction of Ophelia. There can be no question but that this is madness. It moves her to express the plaintive queries that have gone unasked while she was sane: 'How should I your true-love know . . . ?' (IV.v.23). As she sings, her quavering ditties modulate from one loss to another, from lover to father: 'And will he not come again?' (190). Her own death, which occasions further debate, points the plot toward its Fifth-Act destination, where the stage becomes a graveyard and the trap her grave. In the phraseology of Claudius, the play has started from 'dirge in marriage'; it subsides with 'mirth in funeral' (I.ii.12). Tragic laughter has never resounded to the rhythms of a more frenetic *danse macabre*. The two Clowns, who are digging the grave, are shrewd peasants who will not accept a coroner's verdict unquestioningly. The upshot of their own inquest is *se offendendo*. Here they confuse the plea of *se defendendo*, not unmeaningfully, with the theme of offence. The Second Gravedigger is not far from the truth when he maintains that Ophelia killed herself in self-defense. John Donne, in his treatise on suicide, *Biathanatos*, considered that legal question and pronounced it 'perplexed and captious.'

The somber legend of Hamlet has been traced back to an enigma in the Old Norse Eddas; and in the play, as Dover Wilson notes, the very first line of Hamlet's part is a riddle. But it is the First Gravedigger who propounds the ultimate conundrum: 'Who builds stronger than a mason, a shipwright, or a carpenter?' (V.i.57–8). His pride in his profession, which delves for dwellings to outlast all mortal enterprise, emerges with his answer: 'a grave-maker' (65). As he digs, he wheezes out a conventional Tudor song, which juxtaposes youth with age and love with renunciation. Hamlet plies him with professional questions, most of them pertaining to local circumstance, but one possessing a human element of universal interest: 'How long will a man lie i'th' earth ere he rot?' (179). Contemplating the skulls as they are exhumed, Hamlet's satirical imagination restores them to the various ranks of society. This one might have been a politician, he muses, or else a courtier. Where are the lawyer's technicalities or the landlord's documents? he murmurs to Horatio. *Ubi sunt?* The Gravedigger, by identifying one particular skull with that of the late King's late jester, stages a posthumous recognition-scene. 'Where be your gibes now?' Hamlet asks Yorick, his gorge rising, '... your songs? your flashes of merriment ... ? Not one now, to mock your own grinning?' (208–10). And does not the same necessity hold sway over kings and beggars, over Alexander and Caesar as well as Yorick? Hamlet's inquiries, as to the grave's future occupant, have been put off by the Gravedigger's equivocations. When the funeral procession comes to a halt, he recognizes 'who is to be buried,' and his generalities about death are brought home with a shocking particularity.

Hamlet's starting-point has been a death-wish: 'O that this too too sullied flesh would melt ... !' (I.ii.129) Acting out that wish symbolically, he now leaps into the grave, grapples with Laertes, and calls upon the earth to cover them both. After all the postponements and concealments, the conflict is in the open; thundering challenges are exchanged, which eventuate in the final passage at arms. Preliminary arrangements are conducted through a last interlude of light burlesque, a verbalistic combat or guessing-game between Hamlet and Osric. Now that Polonius is out of the way, this new character represents the courtly affectations; more functionally, he is the referee to whom the doubtful points of the duel are submitted. What was to have been a brotherly match soon oversteps the limits of his punctilio. Thanks to the complot of Claudius and Laertes, the outcome is fatal for both duelists, and for Gertrude as well as the King himself. To this reckoning must be added the execution of Rosencrantz and Guildenstern, imminently to be announced by the English Ambassadors, not to mention the deaths of Ophelia and Polonius or the casualty that originally gave us the Ghost. When Fortinbras arrives from his Polish conquest, his Danish inheritance is guaranteed by the disappearance of rival claimants. 'O proud death,' he exclaims as he views the four corpses,

> What feast is toward in thine eternal cell
> That thou so many princes at a shot
> So bloodily hast struck? (v.ii.376–8)

The metaphor accords with the style of a Scandinavian prince, who can envisage dead warriors feasting in Valhalla; it may also recall to us that, in the Viking chronicle, Hamlet confounds his enemies at a banquet. The lone survivor who can explain 'this bloody question' to Fortinbras and the Ambassadors is Horatio; and he will complete the duties of friendship by telling the world 'How these things came about' (386, 391). So far as they can be clarified in terms of human agency, he will speak 'Of carnal, bloody, and unnatural acts,' acts of Claudius involving Gertrude and the Ghost; 'Of accidental judgments, casual slaughters,' claiming as their victims Laertes, Polonius, and Ophelia; 'Of deaths put on by cunning and forc'd cause,' those of Rosencrantz and Guildenstern and of Hamlet himself (392–4).

Horatio would accompany his friend, were it not for a stronger obligation to vindicate Hamlet's fame. Horatio's stoic disposition steels him to attempt what Hamlet himself has avoided, to seek deliberately what Ophelia finds inadvertently, self-slaughter. He must forgo that recourse; yet we must conclude that, if it would have brought him 'felicity,' then felicity must be oblivion; for suicide is not a sanctioned path to a Christian heaven. 'The rest is silence,' Hamlet breaks off; and 'rest' has the added shading of repose, repose to the music–

Horatio hopes—of angels (369–71). 'There is something in this more than natural,' something preternatural if not supernatural; and Hamlet has hoped that 'philosophy could find it out' (III.ii.384–5). But, as he was bound to surmise after seeing and hearing the Ghost, there are more things in heaven and earth than he and Horatio could have conceivably learned from the study of natural philosophy, the scientific curriculum at Wittenberg (I.v.166–7). Hamlet has spoken of his soul as immortal; but he has also spoken of death as an 'undiscover'd country' whence 'No traveller returns' (III.i.79–80). That assumption, taken literally, would discredit the Ghost; and, even if we make an exception for it, its account of its prison house could hardly be more mysterious. In that respect it differs strikingly from the ghost in *The Spanish Tragedy*, whose graphic description of the underworld is recognizable as a classic Elysium. This figure and its companion, an explicit personification of revenge, leave no doubt as to their essential paganism. They have more light to throw upon *Hamlet*, of which Kyd's tragedy is the closest surviving adumbration, than we can gain from the obscurities and inconsistencies of contemporaneous tracts on spiritualism.

Another suggestive analogue might be the more authentically Spanish drama about Don Juan, *The Scoffer of Seville* by Tirso de Molina. There the guest of stone is pressed for details as to 'the other life': what its landscape is like, and whether it harbors any taverns or prizes for poetry. Meanwhile a group of singers chants the fleeting joys of this life, whereas at the finale they hymn the last judgment. Don Juan seems more intransigent in his skepticism than Hamlet; yet, facing the flames, he recants and begs his unrelenting host for a chance to confess and be absolved. The worldview of medieval orthodoxy, which he has called so flagrantly into question, reasserts itself through a naïve miracle. By contradistinction, *Hamlet* takes place in an open universe; its signs and omens, though evident, are equivocal; and it is not merely Claudius, it is Hamlet and nearly everyone else, who dies cut off from confession and absolution, 'Not shriving time allow'd' (v.ii.47). Death is sudden and birth unsought for; the conditions of existence are questionable from first to last; nothing is certain except that churchyards yawn and gravedigging is a useful employment. Yorick's grin is the sole retort to Hamlet's *ubi sunt.* Where indeed are they now, those travelers to the undiscovered country? Only the Ghost can say, and it will not. But it will haunt us all the more, because it materializes 'the dread of something after death,' because it prefigures our vague apprehension of godhead (III.i.78). And we must acknowledge its effect, with the skeptic Horatio, 'It harrows me with fear and wonder" (I.i.44), or with Hamlet himself, 'O wonderful' (I.v.118). Pity and fear are the usual tragic components; but here, while Fortinbras surveys the damage, Horatio bespeaks the emotions of 'woe or wonder' (v.ii.374). The play has kept us guessing; it leaves us wondering.

It does not solve the problem of knowledge, the epistemological question, stated by the Ghost—for our incidental benefit—'tropically.' Rather, we are impelled toward the problem of action, the ethical question, through the trope of revenge. The protracted inquest over the dead King reaches its eventual solution; strategy is met by counter-strategy in a battle of wits confounding the guilty and appalling the innocent. But that is less than half the exciting story, which, if it were not worked out so exhaustively, would be a detective thriller and little more. Shakespeare's development makes it a mystery in the more highly speculative sense, a rite of initiation to painful experience, an exploration of stages of consciousness which dazzle and elude the spectator 'With thoughts beyond the reaches of our souls' (I.iv.56). These are not to be overtaken by criticism—though perhaps, like Horatio and Marcellus after Hamlet and the Ghost, we may follow at a safe and respectful distance. It is the quest and not the object that counts, with Goethe's *Faust*. With *Hamlet*, 'why' and 'wherefore' are brushed aside, as the interrogative gives way to the imperative, 'what should we do?' The first-person plural supports the suggestions, put forward by Hazlitt and endorsed by other perceptive critics, that our interest in the protagonist is a self-involvement; that we are Hamlet. His circumstances are ours, to the extent that every man, in some measure, is born to privilege and anxiety, committed where he has never been consulted, hemmed in on all sides by an overbearing situation, and called upon to perform what must seem an ungrateful task. No wonder he undertakes it with many misgivings, tests it with much groping and some backsliding, pursues it with revisions and indecisions, and parses every affirmation by the grammar of doubt.

THE QUESTION OF HAMLET

II. DOUBT

DRama in outline, as we run no danger of forgetting, can be little more than a student's paradigm of drama in the round. Lambs' *Tales from Shakespeare* show a closer kinship to Grimms' *Fairy Tales* than to the plays that they so blandly recount. Voltaire utilized a synopsis of *Hamlet* as a *reductio ad absurdum* in his notorious attack on Shakespeare. Yet when we have a chance to walk through the script, pausing here and there on our pedestrian tour for brief citations, we may notice elements of design which frequently get lost in actual performance. The most exciting part of the story, Hamlet's journey by sea and fight with pirates, must be narrated at a second and a third remove. What is more unfortunate, these narrations are usually cut on the stage, with a weakening effect upon our impression of Hamlet's character. Not that Hamlet's character is slighted by the actors who star in our theaters; his lines, constituting almost forty per cent of the text, are subject to abridgement less than the rest of it. On the other hand, the seven soliloquies, massive as they may seem when detached from their context, do not constitute much more than five per cent of the whole. Theatrical bowdlerization tends to reduce the dialogue, thereby concentrating the monologue, and underlining the romantic notion of a statuesque figure who broods apart, who thinks too much, who shies away from the others. But Hamlet questions the others as well as himself. He is the chief participant in a dynamic series of oral encounters, though they end by isolating him all the more. All too often we view the play as an opera, awaiting the famous set-pieces as if they were arias, and overlooking the dramatic tensions in the give-and-take of the recitative.

In reconsidering *Hamlet*, we cannot pretend that we are unaware of what happens next or how it all comes out. Knowing what will finally be decided, critics have grown impatient over its agonies of decision, and have blamed Hamlet for undue procrastination. But what may be a foregone conclusion to them must be an open question to him, as we have reminded ourselves by watching the process unfold, and observing how the tone is set through the interaction of questions, answers, and unanswered speculations. Having rehearsed the play once with an emphasis on the interrogative mood, let us push the interrogation further by returning to certain indicative passages, tracing now an inner train of thought, and later placing it in a broader perspective. *Interrogatio* is classified—by the rhetorician, Henry Peacham—as a form of *pathopoeia*, which in turn is neither more nor less than a device for arousing emotions: 'Examples hereof are common in Tragedies.' *Dubitatio*, our next figure of speech and thought, is less emotional and more deliberative. As it is defined by Abraham Fraunce, in *The Arcadian Rhetorike*, 'Addubitation or doubting is a kinde of deliberation with our selues.' The orator deliberates between rival options: either to revenge or not to revenge, whether a visitant comes from heaven or hell. For doubt is that state of mind where the questioner faces no single answer nor the lack of one, but rather a choice between a pair of alternatives. Etymologically, the word stems from *dubitare*, which means precisely to hesitate in the face of two possibilities. The structure of *Hamlet* seems, at every level, to have been determined by this duality. 'A double blessing is a double grace' (I.iii.53).

Similarly, the texture is characterized by a tendency to double and redouble words and phrases. From the very first scene, the speeches abound in hendiadys: 'gross and scope,' 'law and heraldry.' Sometimes the paired nouns are redundant synonyms: 'food and diet,' 'pith and moment'—Saxon balancing Latin as in the doublets of Sir Thomas Browne. Adjectives or verbs are coupled at other times: 'impotent and bedrid,' 'countenance and excuse.' This reduplication seems to be a habit of courtly diction into which Hamlet himself falls now and then: 'the purpose of playing . . . is . . . to show . . . the very age and body of the time his form and pressure' (III.ii.21–5). By the count of R. A. Foakes, no less than 247 such pairings are scattered through the play. They are doubtless more ornamental than functional; yet they charge the air with overtones of wavering and indecision. The Clown goes farther with his equivocations, putting his finger on serious ambiguities. And Hamlet goes too far with his *double-entendres*, besmirching the maidenly innocence of Ophelia. Claudius, in his opening address to the Council, establishes himself as a practiced exponent of stately double-talk. With unctuous skill, he manages a transition from the old King's death to himself and his inherited queen. Antithesis is condensed into oxymoron: 'delight and dole,' 'defeated joy.' Some of these mannerisms will have their echo in the stilted language of the Play-King: 'Grief joys, joy grieves, on slender accident' (III.ii.209). The formal style is a mask, which accords with the dress and etiquette of the court; Claudius is virtually winking, when he speaks of 'an auspicious and a dropping eye' (I.ii.11). Hamlet, speaking informally and ironically to Horatio, sums up the paradoxical situation:

> The funeral bak'd meats
> Did coldly furnish forth the marriage tables. (180–81)

The incrimination of Claudius by the Ghost, duly recorded

in the book of Hamlet's brain, is an object-lesson in duplicity. Claudius himself is unremittingly conscious of the distinction between the 'exterior' and 'the inward man' (II.ii.6). Both in communing with himself and in dealing with others, he seldom fails to distinguish between words and deeds, or face and heart. He introduces Gertrude by publicly casting her in a dual role, 'our sometime sister, now our queen,' as he does his nephew shortly afterward, 'my cousin Hamlet, and my son' (I.ii.8, 64). Hamlet resentfully picks up the implications, and caustically refers to his 'uncle-father and aunt-mother' (II.ii.392). On the premise that 'man and wife is one flesh,' he perversely carries the logic of incest to its conclusion by bidding farewell to Claudius as his 'dear mother' (IV.iii.51). He prefaces his interview with Gertrude by resolving to act a part: 'My tongue and soul in this be hypocrites' (III.ii.415). He will 'speak daggers' to her, and she will admit that his words are 'like daggers' (III.iv.95). Addressing her as 'your husband's brother's wife,' he implores her to keep aloof from Claudius, though she may feel otherwise inclined: 'Assume a virtue, if you have it not' (15, 160). It is the recommendation of worldly wisdom that La Rochefoucauld would moralize: 'Hypocrisy is the tribute that vice pays to virtue.' Molière's *Misanthrope* would reject such sophistications; Alceste stands squarely for virtue disdaining vice; like the ingenuous Hamlet, he knows not 'seems.' But Hamlet, unlike Alceste, learns to live at court, in an arena where men and women must be actors and actresses. He must learn an etymology which may not have struck him during his humanistic studies at Wittenberg—that the word 'hypocrite,' in the original Greek, designated an actor.

Claudius, invoking the 'twofold force' of prayer, acknowledges his own hypocrisy, caught as he is between guilt and repentance:

> . . . like a man to double business bound,
> I stand in pause where I should first begin. (III.iii.41–2)

A moment later, Hamlet will stand in pause before the double business of whether Claudius should be saved or damned, and will give him the benefit of an unforeseen doubt. The smiling villain is a double-dealer; but so is Hamlet, in another sense. At the beginning he is single-minded, all of a piece, all melancholia; then he puts on his mask and plays the antic, carrying his buffoonery to the verge of hysteria; his disposition is manic in the presence of others and depressive when he is by himself. Where the vicious Claudius assumes an air of respectability, the virtuous Hamlet must assimilate the atmosphere of licentiousness. He must set aside the high-minded idealism of Castiglione's *Courtier*, 'The courtier's, scholar's, soldier's eye, tongue, sword,' and take up the time-serving realism of Machiavelli's *Prince* (III.i.159). It is the role of Polonius, as chamberlain, to profess the one and practice the other. While he privately expounds a philosophy of keeping up appearances, he prides himself on his capacity for seeing through them. Master of ceremonies, he bustles about, arranging formalities according to protocol; but he is also a master of palace intrigue, who sneaks behind curtains to spy; and, with him, the play oscillates between ceremonious public hearings and furtive whisperings behind the scenes, so to speak. With the twin figures of Rosencrantz and Guildenstern, the double-dealing is symmetrically personified. Since they invariably hunt in couples, their roles are interchangeable. Each of them has an introductory speech of exactly the same length and rhythm, and in each case the key-word is 'both' (II.ii.26–32).

> Thanks, Rosencrantz and gentle Guildenstern,

the King responds, and the Queen preserves the symmetry by adding:

Thanks, Guildenstern and gentle Rosencrantz.

Hamlet's singleness and singularity set him off from this duplication and conformity on the part of his schoolfellows. His tragic solitude is emphasized by the comic aspect of their behavior, as they vie with each other in flattering the King and the Queen or in evading the Prince. 'I am most dreadfully attended,' he complains, meaning that he is badly served—and, more intimately, that he is haunted by a ghost (II.ii.275–6). Well may he jest with Rosencrantz and Guildenstern about the harlotry of the goddess Fortune, since they are turning out to be fortune-seekers, royal spies, and unfaithful friends. Yet he retains one true friend, who is a Damon to his Pythias, equally impervious to 'Fortune's buffets and rewards'; and in that short, rare, half-embarrassed interim of sincerity between his advice to the Players and their play, Hamlet praises Horatio because he is not 'a pipe for Fortune's finger/ To sound what stop she please' (III.ii.72, 75–6). After 'The Mousetrap' has been sprung, with Horatio counterspying upon Claudius, Hamlet calls for recorders and enacts his metaphor with Rosencrantz and Guildenstern. Fortune's finger may sound their stops, but they cannot pluck out the heart of his mystery. ' 'Sblood, do you think I am easier to be play'd on than a pipe?' (384–5). And, having told them off, having demonstrated his own virtuosity by plucking out the mystery of Claudius, he continues the music-lesson by teasing Polonius, who can be played on like any courtly instrument. Within a confused and crowded hour, the elderly politician is dead, and Hamlet is being hustled off to England, dreadfully attended by Rosencrantz and Guildenstern. When he turns back to challenge Claudius, Hamlet will be unarmed—as he writes in his letter, 'naked'—and, as he adds in a postscript, 'alone' (IV.vii.52–3).

It is this isolation from all the others, this alienation from his environment, that has made Hamlet the spiritual patron of many a disinherited modern hero. He has a confidant, to be sure, in Horatio; but Horatio, in spite of his devotion, can hardly do more than echo Hamlet's dubieties. Involved in a complex and subtle network of human relations, all of them strained, Hamlet sees himself 'benetted round with villanies' (V.ii.29). His father is dead through suspected foul play; his mother has remarried under dubious and technically immoral circumstances; his uncle, to whom he is naturally antipathetic, would seem to be culpable on both of those counts. Love, between Hamlet and Ophelia, is an excluded possibility from the very first time it is mentioned; we hear of it mainly from the other side, through a series of warnings and farewells; and it is from Ophelia's grave that Hamlet dares at last to avow what might have been. Laertes imprecates him with 'treble woe' (V.i.269); for Ophelia, too, has been triply isolated; cut off and crazed by her lover's defection, her brother's absence and her father's accident, she could do nothing but wander to muddy death. Thus family ties are broken while, on the plane of the state, the social order is jeopardized internally and externally. 'The people muddied,' Laertes makes his appearance as the leader of their revolt (IV.v.81). The invasion of Denmark by Norway under Fortinbras, long threatened and averted earlier, becomes a virtual conquest by default. These mishaps, domestic and dynastic, have their counterparts in that cosmic disorder of which the Ghost is the portent. It heralds the anarchy that we behold. It presupposes a chaos which is left, with darkling hints, to our imagination.

This world, in Hamlet's opening description, is 'an unweeded garden' (I.ii.135). Well-tended gardens always stand for the norms of nature in Shakespeare's imagery; here the blight is traceable not merely to neglect, but to a kind of perverse cultivation; and Gertrude will be cautioned by Hamlet against spreading compost on the weeds (III.iv.151). The Ghost is manifestly a sign that something is rotten; more problematically, it points a course of action for setting things right. By obeying its supernatural behest, Hamlet might solve the political and personal problems at one fell swoop, removing his uncle from his father's throne and from his mother's bed. But, having been led to question all that seems most familiar, how can he be expected to trust the unknown? Hence, according to James Russell Lowell, 'Hamlet doubts everything.' Doubt is 'The beacon of the wise,' says Hector in *Troilus and Cressida;* moreover, it is a probe for the wounded, 'the tent that searches/ To th' bottom of the worst.' It is the rhetorical pattern that formulates the philosophical outlook of skepticism. By Sir Walter Ralegh's definition, 'The Skeptick doth neither affirm, nor denie any Position; but doubteth of it.' And since a skeptic is by derivation an onlooker, his doubts are hesitations. As a doubter, Hamlet cannot be considered idiosyncratic; his consciousness that the time is out of joint was widely shared by late Elizabethans. Experimental science, 'New Philosophy,' as John Donne was lamenting, 'calls all in doubt.' The well-ordered cosmos of Ptolemaic astronomy was being displaced by the planetary system of Copernicus, wherein the sun no longer revolved around the earth and man was no longer the center of creation. So Hamlet could write to Ophelia:

> Doubt thou the stars are fire;
> Doubt that the sun doth move;
> Doubt truth to be a liar;
> But never doubt I love. (II.ii.116–19)

As a poet who mixes cosmology with intimacy, Hamlet obviously belongs to the Metaphysical School. The purport of his stanza does not differ much from the conclusion of Arnold's 'Dover Beach,' the affirmation that, in a universe of illusion and pain, the only true relationship is love. But Hamlet recants his love soon afterward, while Ophelia herself is enveloped from first to last in an astral nimbus of uncertainty. Her first speech, in response to her brother's parting request, is the question, 'Do you doubt that?' (I.iii.4). Her last rites are curtailed by the Priest because 'Her death was doubtful' (V.i.250). The tenderness of lovers can be no more than a trivial fond record which Hamlet must erase from his tablets of memory. Only the filial relationship can retain its meaning for him; and it is, to put it mildly, a peculiar one; for he is not the son and heir of his father so much as the son and revenger of a ghost; he is, we might deduce, the incarnate member of an unhallowed trinity. It may be significant that, although the late King was called Horwendill in the chronicle, he too is named Hamlet in the play. The name is introduced with reference to him, 'our valiant Hamlet,' whereas no one refers to 'young Hamlet' until the closing lines of the introductory scene. (I.i.84, 170). 'Young Fortinbras' has already come under discussion as the son of old King Fortinbras, who was slain and whose Norwegian army was defeated by the elder Hamlet. The invidious parallel will be clinched by the fact that the younger Hamlet was born on the day of his father's victory; and that was the day, as we shall likewise discover, when the Gravedigger started to ply his callous trade (V.i.156–7).

Though the part of the Ghost is dignified by our awareness that Shakespeare appeared in it, though it has its portentous harangue, it is confined to four scenes and is mute in two of them. Yet it is omnipresent, *hic et ubique*. Like the defunct Captain Alving in Ibsen's *Ghosts*, Hamlet the Elder dominates the lives of those who have survived him. The opening scene evokes the recollection of his military exploits against Poland and Norway; the attempt to identify him particularizes, one by one in the mind's eye, his physical characteristics; the harangue includes a first-hand account of his bodily dissolution after his poisoning. The disembodied presence that emerges is fully armed, wearing a beaver and bearing a truncheon, with grizzled beard and sorrowful countenance: an awesome figure of heroic proportions. 'Remember me' is his hollow farewell from the battlement (I.v.91). And, in the Queen's closet, he objurgates, 'Do not forget' (III.iv.110). Claudius and Gertrude, of course, would urge the consolations of forgetfulness, that decaying weed of Lethe wharf. In their funereal commonplaces, they point out that the death of parents is not a unique but a universal bereavement, and that every father has lost a father before him back to the origins of the race. This line of reasoning proves to be a better warrant for Hamlet's cult of remembrance, for the qualms of succession he feels as a son, the child's reluctance to grow up, the youth's assumption that an intervening generation protects him from death. Looking backward toward those bygone fathers who have been sons in their time, Hamlet can envision the Ghost as an archetypal forbear, as our composite ancestry, the dead hand of the past, the constraining weight of tradition.

The roots of Hamlet's story, like those of Beowulf's, go deep into the bleak and marshy soil of Norse folklore. It comes down to us from the sagas of the Vikings, out of darker ages into the Renaissance, through a process of literary recension elaborate and sensitive enough to have been finally influenced by Montaigne. Shakespeare's immediate source, the French collection of *Histoires tragiques* by Belleforest, comments upon the barbarity of Scandinavian customs as exemplified in the tale. In that tragical history there was no need to conceal the slaying, and consequently no secret to impart by supernatural means. The Ghost, with its lugubrious refrain, 'Hamlet, revenge!', seems to have been the most popular adjunct of an earlier and cruder dramatic version than Shakespeare's. Shakespeare refined upon this material by surrounding it with mystery. Skillful adapter that he was, he exploited its very resistance to adaptation. He showed revenge as a harsh and brutal convention, more honored in the breach than in the observance. He seems to have understood how a legend can owe its strength to survival, how its encrustations and stratifications can recapitulate the traditional stages of cultural development, and how its inherent discrepancies can dramatize a conflict between primitive instinct and civilized restraint. This conflict, as between the two Hamlets, may be respectively symbolized by the soldier's truncheon and the scholar's book. The lapse of a generation separates them, dating from the defeat of Fortinbras, as well as from the Play-King's marriage, just thirty years ago. How exactly that same round number marks Hamlet's age would seem to vary with our confidence in the Gravedigger's roundabout testimony. Most readers prefer to visualize a younger Hamlet; most actors are bound to present a somewhat older one.

'Must I remember?' Hamlet has asked himself, before the Ghost has answered for him in the imperative (I.ii.143). Could he ever forget? Back in his study at Wittenberg, could the young intellectual have escaped from the shade of the dead hero, and have ceased to measure himself—man and boy—by the father-image? His uncle-father is no more like Hamlet the Elder 'Than I to Hercules,' Hamlet the Younger declares (153). Thereby he disparages his own prowess, along with that of his father's successor, who has rebuked him for 'unmanly grief' (94). Whatever his inclination, he is not allowed to lead the contemplative life; he must be active, willy-nilly; and to avenge his father would, in effect, be to step into his father's shoes. 'Let Hercules himself do what he may,' nevertheless every dog will have his proverbial day, and the Younger will somehow come into his own (v.i.315). But his Herculean standards will still be set by the past glories of the warrior King. With all his imperfections, all the Elder's faults, the defects of his soldierly virtues, he remains the embodiment of mankind in the fullness of manhood.

> He was a man, take him for all in all.
> I shall not look upon his like again. (I.ii. 187–8)

Soon after pronouncing this kingly epitaph, as irony will have it, Hamlet will look upon the paternal likeness again. Whether that phantom is animated by an immortal soul or by an evil genius will be the doubt that continues to trouble Hamlet, as he threads his way between shadows and substances, trying to discriminate spirit from matter. 'The body is with the King, but the King is not with the body' (IV.ii.28–9). Hamlet's ambiguous relation to his father is mirrored by the ambiguous identity of the Ghost in the background. Both are related to the ambiguity in the foreground, the strategic role of the two-faced Claudius and the running contrast between his person and that of his predecessor, more than kin, less than kind.

The link between man and man, ideally, is brotherhood. Here it has been subverted into fratricide, the underlying offence, as the offending brother keenly discerns in his self-examination: 'It hath the primal eldest curse upon't' (III.iii.37). It came into the world, bringing death along with it, in direct consequence to the original sin of our ultimate parents. Hence, when the Gravedigger turns up the first of his skulls, Hamlet regards it 'as if 'twere Cain's jawbone' (V.i.84–5). Although the sinful Claudius is branded by that Biblical prototype, his more humane brother attracts comparisons of a more classical sort, such as the implied resemblance to Hercules. The fraternal antipathy is stated, in Hamlet's First Soliloquy, by the equation: 'Hyperion to a satyr' (I.ii.140). True royalty is, appropriately, a sun-god; the sensual interloper is a goatish caricature of a human being; and that polarity stretches, across the whole scale of creation, from the superhuman to the subhuman. Hamlet's allusion to the sun breeding maggots in a dead dog, 'being a god kissing carrion,' is a prose variation upon the same theme (II.ii.182). But, in this instance, fleshly weakness takes the shape of mortality rather than sensuality. Both themes are interconnected through, for example, the monologue of the Ghost, which proceeds from the carnal to the charnel, from the falling-off of the Queen to the after-effects of the poison. Gertrude, for her failure to observe the proprieties of mourning, has been invidiously compared to 'a beast that wants—' and the phrase describing what it is that differentiates men from beasts was originally Montaigne's—'discourse of reason' (I.ii.150). The allegation becomes a generalization in Hamlet's Seventh Soliloquy, which examines the uses and the abuses of reason:

> What is a man,
> If his chief good and market of his time
> Be but to sleep and feed? A beast, no more. (IV.iv.33–5)

Gods are invoked to canonize men at their best, animals to stigmatize men at their worst. Improvising doggerel after the play, Hamlet likens his father to the ruler of the gods, 'Jove himself' (III.ii.294). The epithet for his uncle, preordained by the rhyme, is 'ass'; but Hamlet, in high spirits, substitutes 'pajock' or peacock. Later epithets are less flattering—paddock, bat, gib, ape (III.iv.190; IV.ii.18). Claudius is envisaged calling Gertrude his 'mouse,' and wallowing in 'an enseamed bed' with her like two pigs in a sty (III.iv.92). A nobleman, an Osric, may be 'a beast'; but if he is also a 'lord of beasts,' if he possesses land and livestock, others will be as obsequious to him as he is to the royal family (V.ii.88). Such is the way of the world, though it mystifies Hamlet. During the reign of the elder Hamlet, people made faces at Claudius; now that he is enthroned, they pay large sums for his 'picture in little' (II.ii.384). This comment is elicited by the popularity of the child-actors, which has driven the Players away from their city, where they performed under the sign of Hercules. Having been dispossessed, they are entertained at Elsinore with some warmth of fellow-feeling by Hamlet. His association of ideas, linking their theatrical competition to his obsession with his stepfather, foreshadows the Closet Scene—or, more specifically, the Portrait Scene, where Gertrude is violently confronted by Hamlet with a pair of miniatures, pictures in little of both her husbands.

> Look here upon this picture, and on this,
> The counterfeit presentment of two brothers. (III.iv.53–4)

Using the rhetorical figure known as *icon* or verbal portraiture, a favorite Shakespearean embellishment, Hamlet portrays his father at full length and in Olympian majesty. It is an idealized portrait, a classicized image in the Renaissance manner, combining 'Hyperion's curls' with Jove's forehead, the eye of Mars, and the posture of Mercury:

> A combination and a form indeed
> Where every god did seem to set his seal
> To give the world assurance of a man. (60–62)

Hamlet's depiction is almost a conjuration, inasmuch as it seems to raise the Ghost, 'My father, in his habit as he liv'd'—not in armor now, but in the very gown he must have worn on his previous visits to this chamber (135). But Gertrude is blind to him; while Hamlet goes on to sketch a companion portrait, denouncing the bloated Claudius as 'A king of shreds and patches,' a sexual and a political usurper (102). The brothers are as dissimilar in stature as in merit; indeed, they are like mountain and moor; the one is not worth the twentieth part of the tithe of the other. 'What judgment,' Hamlet passionately demands of his mother, 'Would step from this to this?' (70–71).

Even the exuberant Host in *The Merry Wives of Windsor* wavers, for a moment, 'in perplexity and doubtful dilemma.' So the thoughtless Gertrude, all too briefly transfixed by Hamlet's pictorial exhibit, achieves a reluctant glimpse of self-discovery and moral discrimination. However, the interrupted recognition-scene has a much broader significance. Turning in the other direction, Hamlet holds—as it were—the portraits up to his audience. By that express gesture, he brings the intrinsic dualism of the play to its climactic statement, while Shakespeare confronts the age and body of the time with the form and pressure of its greatest doubt. What is a man . . . ? The sustained inquiry still re-echoes after the final soliloquy, to be intermittently resumed in *King Lear* and *Macbeth*. Such was the anxious question of Old Testament ethics, voiced by the Psalmist: 'What is man, that thou art mindful of him?' Sophocles propounded the confident answer of humanism, when the chorus in *Antigone* praised mankind as the wonder of wonders, controlling the world through his works, led by his ingenuity toward both good and evil, capable of meeting all situations save death. Those may well have been the preconditions of tragedy for Hamlet the Elder; he was a man, to say the very least. It is his long-drawn-out eulogy and his difficult testament that lay down the preconditions of tragedy for Hamlet the Younger. The latter reveals his training as a humanist when he exclaims: 'What a piece of work is a man!' But the exclamation, we have noted, has an undertone of interrogation. Hamlet utters the sentiment in order to qualify it, shifting his focus from the potentialities to the limitations of the species. If man is a matchless creature, he is 'the paragon of animals.' To complete that paradox, he is the last refinement, the 'quintessence of dust' (II.ii.316–17).

Man, according to medieval Christian tradition, occupies a middle status within the great chain of being. Created in the divine image out of dust, lower than the angels and higher than the brutes, equally endowed with godlike capabilities and bestial appetites, he may elevate or debase himself through the exercise of his will. But the Renaissance held a challenge to this scheme of things, as it did to hierarchies and settled beliefs in other spheres of culture and society. The unifying but limiting synthesis tended to break down into two conflicting positions, which Theodore Spencer has suggestively outlined in his study of Shakespeare's ideas. Changing attitudes toward human nature, as expressed by thinkers of the period, oscillate between theological and naturalistic extremes. At one extreme is the 'Oration on the Dignity of Man' by Pico della Mirandola, with its lofty plea for man's self-liberation through his intellectual and spiritual faculties. At the opposite pole is Montaigne's 'Apology for Ramón Sabunde,' with its devastating critique of the senses and of man's consequent frailties and confusions. Man's quandary, in choosing between these polar conceptions of himself, has been aptly set forth by the laureate of antithesis, Alexander Pope:

> . . . in doubt to act or rest;
> In doubt to deem himself a god, or beast;
> In doubt his mind or body to prefer;
> Born but to die, and reas'ning but to err.

This, in the largest sense, is the alternative that Shakespeare places before us through the contrasting pictures of two kings, the slain protector and the menacing slayer. For the Queen, more immediately, the issue is between two ways of living, which she has adopted in promiscuous succession. For Hamlet, the decision is suspended between what was and what is, what should be and what has become intolerable, between an archetype of the good life which is the merest shadow of its former self and an embodiment of malefaction which is substantial, successful, and authoritative. Friar Lawrence, in *Romeo and Juliet*, extracts the same lesson from plants:

> Two such opposed kings encamp them still
> In man as well as herbs—grace and rude will.

Hamlet's discontent with man is generic, though the incredulous smiles of Rosencrantz and Guildenstern seemed to imply that woman might please him better. To be specific, in his First Soliloquy, he has identified frailty with womanhood; and he keeps up a misogynistic barrage which hits its target in the Closet Scene. By holding up his dramatic mirror to Claudius, he has just exposed man's depravity. Now, by setting up 'a glass' wherein Gertrude may behold 'the inmost part' of herself, he is exposing woman's culpability (III.iv.19–20). The locale is appropriate to the exposure, if the Queen's closet serves as her dressing-room, where presumably she applies cosmetics. Therefore the looking-glass may have its literal place in the scene, while it symbolically links acting with painting as metaphors of hypocrisy. Artifice, as an aid to beauty, is a standard topic of anti-feminine satire. 'God hath given you one face, and you make yourselves another,' Hamlet sneers incongruously during his one scene with Ophelia, having satirized the follies of dotage during his earlier scene with Polonius (III.i.148–9). A vignette of my lady in her chamber, painting an inch thick, is the culminating example of earthly vanity to which Hamlet juxtaposes the skull of Yorick. Claudius draws another explicit moral, in his most revealing aside; his misdeed, glossed over by his 'painted word,' is like a 'harlot's cheek, beautied with plast'ring art' (51–3). Polonius, we might recall, objected to the word 'beautified' in the letter that Hamlet addressed to Ophelia—and we might further recall that the participle once had carried a special sting for Shakespeare, when Robert Greene had castigated him as an upstart crow, beautified with the feathers of elder and better playwrights.

For Polonius, the objectionable implication is the nuance between 'beautified' and 'beautiful,' the suspicion that his daughter may owe her loveliness to plastering art, that her beauty is as delusive as her honesty, that she is a painted woman. Obviously, she is nothing of the kind; *honi soit qui mal y pense;* and Rebecca West's recent attempt to blacken her character does not speak very charitably for Miss West. While the other characters play their double games, the simple Ophelia is halved by loss of reason; she is divided from her judgment, 'Without the which' —as who but Claudius sententiously remarks?—'we are pictures of mere beasts' (IV.v.86). In some respects, the Closet Scene has its rehearsal in the Nunnery Scene, wherein Hamlet's scathing denunciation of femininity might have been more pertinently directed at Gertrude than at Ophelia. This prurient conversation on sex is, again, the immediate sequel to his meditation on death. It is a characteristic transition from the paternal to the maternal area of concern. If man is a sinner, woman can only be 'a breeder of sinners.' Birth can be no blessing; not to be born is best; 'it were better my mother had not borne me' (III.i.122–5). There has been one marriage too many; hereafter there shall be 'no moe marriages.' Gertrude, by her hasty and incestuous remarriage, has profaned a sacrament. Hamlet, in his revulsion, will annul that marriage by killing Claudius; but he will give up the notion of wedlock for himself; and, dog in the manger, he will condemn Ophelia to die a virgin. 'Those that are married already—all but one—shall live; the rest shall keep as they are. To a nunnery, go' (152-4). Take the veil, and let the loveless breed of men and women doom themselves to extinction.

The connection between Gertrude and Claudius, regarded by Hamlet as so unnatural, has the effect of inhibiting normal courtship between himself and Ophelia. Instead, it occasions a sort of emotional displacement, which has easily lent itself to Freudian interpretation. Insofar as it may account for the ambivalent zeal with which he harps upon the connubial embraces of his mother and uncle, this is a relevant consideration. Insofar as the Oedipus complex may be a valid conception of the child's unconscious relationship with its parents, it is applicable to everyone, and not peculiarly to Hamlet. To be sure, Hamlet does not leave Gertrude to heaven; his painful dialogue with her so far exceeds the instructions of the Ghost that it invites psychological theorizing; and the study of the late Ernest Jones is outstanding, among the efforts of psychoanalytic criticism, for the resilience of its argument and for its acquaintance with the subject-matter. It motivates Hamlet's delay by identifying him with Claudius, through whom he has vicariously accomplished the Oedipal feat of murdering his father and marrying his mother. If this be the case, it must be said that Hamlet conceals his sympathy for his uncle from the audience more effectively than he conceals his hostility to, and from, Claudius. In his expressed admiration for his father and in the disgust he displays toward his mother, he seems to have more in common with Orestes than with Oedipus. Certainly, we come closer to Shakespeare's plot with the hero of the *Oresteia*, who is hounded by the Furies if not by a ghost, and who avenges his father's death upon his mother's lover, and upon her as well. The power of such a myth, as Gilbert Murray suggests, may lie in the collective imagination rather than in the individual ego. Yet, the plight of Orestes was not entirely within the family, and his father's murderer was revenging a father of his own.

If brotherhood—the bond between man and man—is degraded in *Hamlet* to fratricide, then love—the bond between man and woman—is perverted to incest. Gertrude may not have been an adulteress during her first husband's lifetime; but she has grossly overstepped a strict barrier by remarrying within the forbidden degrees of kinship. Just as the Portrait Scene presents man at his best and worst, so the two heroines are depicted in opposition to one another, adultery and virginity, the faithless mother and wife versus the faithful daughter and sister. The matron, all too suddenly, has pivoted from a funeral to a nuptial; the maiden, who might well be expecting a nuptial, obtains a sudden funeral. Ophelia's prototype is Jephthah's daughter, the sacrificial victim of ironic mischance. Gertrude's model should be Niobe or Hecuba, the mourning mother or wife; but it is conspicuously not, until the scene where she scatters flowers on Ophelia's grave. Then the bond between woman and woman comes out, her motherly feeling for the motherless girl. Like the momentary flicker of brotherly feeling between Laertes and Hamlet, it is a reminder of the unconsummated romance. The natural freshness of flowers suffuses Ophelia, whereas Gertrude is associated with the artificial enticement of cosmetics. Laertes has begun by warning his sister that Hamlet's love for her will be nipped in the bud, that it is no more than

> A violet in the youth of primy nature,
> Forward, not permanent–sweet, not lasting. (I.iii.7–8)

When she makes her final entrance, mad, she distributes imaginary posies, fitting each presentation to the recipient according to a neatly ordered symbolism. The violets have withered, she laments, on the very day her father died. Both she and Gertrude will wear the flower of pity, 'herb of grace,' but the Queen must wear her 'rue with a difference' (IV.v.181–3). Two scenes later, it is Gertrude who announces Ophelia's death; and the wording of Gertrude's choric speech draws, with touching and delicate sympathy, upon the language of the flowers. The orchid to which she alludes as 'dead men's fingers' has 'a grosser name' which she pointedly avoids (IV.vii.175): it is 'the rampant widow.'

The innocent and corrupted ladies, the good and evil kings: these polarities influence Hamlet's course as clearly as if he were Everyman. But existence is really too complicated a problem to be comprehended within the limits of allegory; and Hamlet is by no means an average hero or *l'homme moyen intellectuel.* He is not only—cursed spite!—a prince, with a deferred heritage and a pressing obligation; he is also—or would rather be—a scholar who has studied philosophy, and whose brain is studiously conceived as a 'book and volume' whereon experience may be registered and analyzed (I.v.103). His preliminary analysis, as we have seen, takes the inevitable form of a sequence of questions. One question leads to another, and all of them bear either upon the supernatural message or upon the cruel mandate. These two crucial issues are doubts, in the technical sense of our term; each is a kind of deliberation with ourselves, as rhetoric would have it, a hesitation before alternatives. Questioning gives the dialogue its pitch of intensity and its rhythm of agitation. Doubting gives pause, brings intervals of suspense, prompts Hamlet to resume his intermittent monologue. The solitary protagonist seems to wander through a labyrinth, wherein every turning-point marks a new predicament before which he must stop to deliberate. The seven soliloquies are, of course, his deliberations. The First of them, relating to his parents, strikes the note of dejection; the Second, reacting to the Ghost, seals a vow; the Third, inspired by the Player, plans a test. The Fifth, coming after the play, is a resolve to chide the Queen; the Sixth, spoken behind the kneeling King, is a postponement of the revenge; the Seventh, spurred by the army of Fortinbras, is a final call to action.

The Fourth and central soliloquy occupies an exceptional

position, both in its context and among the bywords that have winged their way out of literature into life. The generality of its purport has been confirmed by the universality of its appeal. Unlike the other six soliloquies, it does not mention particular events or individuals; nor does it advance the action of the play. Unlike the first three, it does not begin with the interjection, 'O!'. Its tone is quietly meditative, and so detached that the whole episode has been misplaced in the First Quarto, where the Nunnery Scene precedes the Fishmonger Scene. But its obvious place is at the still midpoint of the play. This comes early in Act III and soon after the soliloquy that terminates Act II; Hamlet's part has no lines between these two soliloquies. In the Third, he has expressed his pent-up emotion and arrived at his projected scheme. In the Fourth, while he awaits his opportunity, he is free to consider the most basic of all predicaments. Though he soliloquizes, he is not altogether *solus*, as it happens. Claudius and Polonius, those 'lawful espials,' are watching every move from behind their arras; and there is an ironic disparity between the loftiness of Hamlet's thoughts and the baseness of their suspicions (III.i.32). Furthermore, their decoy, Ophelia, is on stage, reading a book of devotion to 'colour' her 'loneliness'—to serve as a pretext for apparently being unaccompanied. Her sanctimonious father, who could dismiss Hamlet's vows as 'sanctified and pious bawds,' has pushed her into this provocative role (I.iii.130). But Hamlet is too abstracted to be provoked, at least for a while; and her devotional posture, when he does take notice, provokes him to recommend the nunnery.

His loneliness needs no coloring. The convention of the soliloquy, treating his speech as if it were unheard by the other actors, isolates him further from them and brings him closer to us. We are permitted to share the stream of his consciousness. It is a far cry from the oratory of Polonius; hence, to a neo-classicist like Goldsmith, it seemed a 'strange rhapsody of broken images.' But, though the syntax is quite informal, the movement of ideas is logical. If clauses dangle, it is because the speaker interrupts and argues with himself. The process of dubitation, with its disjunctive *eithers* and *whethers*, usually involves more choices than one; and readers or hearers oversimplify when they equate 'to be' with 'to suffer' and 'to take arms' with 'not to be' (III.i.56–8). The method preferred by Renaissance logicians—which does not differ greatly from the selective procedures used today by so-called mechanical brains—was the dichotomy, which chopped its subjects down by dividing them in half and subdividing the resultant divisions into halves again. The result may be bracketed into a diagram of the sort that we find in Robert Burton or Petrus Ramus. Thus, if we leave aside the unpromising consequences of 'not to be,' the proposition 'to be' entails two possibilities: 'to suffer,' and—if we flinch from that for the moment—'to take arms. . .' What follows is, once more, a bifurcation. How we may end our troubles by opposing them is equivocal; our opposition may do away with them or with ourselves. This deflects us toward the alternative, 'to die'; and if that is truly the end, if death is no more than a sleep, we are back in the dreamless realm of 'not to be.' But if, instead of oblivion, there are dreams; and if those dreams are nightmares, comparable to the worst sufferings of this life; then we are impaled upon the other horn of the dilemma—'to suffer . . .', 'to be. . .' (see Figure 1, page 167).

Such is the doubter's mode of dialectic, which leads him back—through complementary semi-circles—to his binary point of departure. That is the question, *esse aut non esse*, which metaphysicians from Plato to Sartre have pondered. Hamlet seeks the essence of things in a world of phenomena, where being must be disentangled from seeming; and since the entanglement is a personal one, perhaps a sword is the only means of escape. The ontological question becomes an existential question, and the argument shifts from metaphysics to ethics. 'Only one philosophical problem is really serious, and that is suicide,' Albert Camus has written. 'To decide whether or not life is worth living is to answer the most fundamental question of philosophy.' Shakespeare explored that problem repeatedly; in his Roman tragedies he condoned, and even ennobled, the Stoic solution. In *Hamlet* a powerful death-wish is suppressed by the Christian canon against self-slaughter. Yet Horatio professes to be more Roman than Danish, in this respect; Ophelia dies by self-offence, in the Gravediggers' verdict; and Hamlet's latent impulse becomes the premise for sweeping generalizations. He has joked about Fortune with Rosencrantz and Guildenstern, and has heard the bitch-goddess cursed by the Player. Must one endure her onslaughts with a Stoic's resignation, Hamlet now asks himself; should one passively submit or actively resist? He envisions himself taking arms not against her weapons, 'slings and arrows,' but in an ill-matched combat with a formless and overwhelming enemy, 'a sea of troubles.' Trouble will come to Claudius like 'the ocean' rushing across 'the flats' (IV.v.99). The Gravedigger will act out the conundrum of whether a man drowns himself or is drowned by the water.

Hamlet's image has been severely criticized, cleverly emended, and evasively translated. It is certainly vulnerable from the standpoint of military tactics. But it need not be taken as a mixed metaphor; it is rather a hyperbole. A warrior marching armed into the sea would be improbable yet impressive, ready to stand beside such indomitable British worthies as King Canute apostrophizing the waves and Mrs. Partington battling the Atlantic. We may take it as a Shakespearean symbol of beleagered humanity in its strife against the overpowering elements, an ineffectual fight in a noble cause. Its outcome is death—what else?—but what, then, is death? Hamlet's clearest answer will be his enigmatic parenthesis:

> The undiscover'd country, from whose bourn
> No traveller returns. (III.i.79–80)

This passage may have been suggested by Marlowe's *Edward II*, when the free-thinking Mortimer dies like a traveler, who 'Goes to discover countries yet unknown.' He is approaching the mystery from which Hamlet draws back. The phrasing of the latter is significantly garbled in the First Quarto, where we are offered an unauthorized and ungrammatical glance at the vista that Shakespeare has carefully veiled from us:

> The undiscover'd country, at whose sight
> The happy smile, and the accursed damn'd.

It is essential to the soliloquy, as it is to the play, that we remain in the dark about the prospective blessings and banes of the afterlife. 'To die—to sleep—' Hamlet stops twice at this precarious equipoise (60, 64). The first time, his abrupt and elliptical 'No more' seems to write off everything else as nothingness; yet it evokes its opposite, Macbeth's 'Sleep no more.' The second time, Hamlet encounters 'the rub,' the obstacle in a metaphorical game of bowls. This is the orthodox hypothesis that death may not be an annihilation but another stage of consciousness. 'To sleep—perchance to dream.' If the discontents of this life are bad dreams, as he has averred to Rosencrantz and Guildenstern, those of the next may be worse; and who shall say which are more real? (II.ii.262). Having arrived at that impasse, Hamlet buttresses it with two searching rhetorical questions, in which the inflection falls upon the verb, 'bear' (III.i.70,76,81). An unsheathed dagger might settle our account in short order; but we prefer the heartache and calamity of staying alive to 'the dread of something after death.' The soliloquy, according to Wilson Knight, 'concentrates on the terrors of an afterlife.'

Yet these are far less concretely in evidence than 'those ills we have,' the evils that flesh is heir to. Like the Duke, sermonizing on death in *Measure for Measure*, Hamlet reasons with life. Shakespeare was always aware of what even Tourneur, in *The Atheist's Tragedy*, fitfully perceived: 'It is not death but life that tries us.'

Life tries Hamlet with the uttermost severity, and that is why he is contemplating death. Yet his decision is in favor of life, even though he sustains it through inaction, while enumerating some of the daily burdens that make it so tragic: oppression, pride, love scorned, merit unrecognized. Erasmus, in *The Praise of Folly*, includes a comparable list of human miseries; a wise man, looking down on that abject panorama from a high place, might well be tempted to self-destruction; wherefore Erasmus concludes with his usual inference, that it is folly to be wise. Hamlet is not unmindful of the fool's wisdom when he puts on his antic disposition. But, in introspection, his mentor is Montaigne; the soliloquies are like the *Essays* in balancing arguments with counter-arguments, in pursuing wayward ideas and unmasking stubborn illusions, in scholarly illustrations and homely afterthoughts which range from the soul of Nero to John-a-dreams. More than with any other theme, Montaigne confides, he has entertained himself with 'imagination of death.' If that is 'a consummation/Devoutly to be wished' for Shakespeare, for him it is 'a consummation of ones being . . . a quiet rest and gentle sleepe, and without dreames.' For him, and often for Shakespeare too, 'We wake sleeping, and sleep waking.' Montaigne's phraseology—or rather, that of his Elizabethan translator, John Florio—reverberates throughout the play. So does Montaigne's philosophy, insofar as it may be said to ramify from his two postulates: '*philosopher c'est apprendre à mourir*' and '*philosopher c'est douter*.' And here it is Montaigne who puts on the antic disposition: 'If, as some say, to philosophate be to doubt; with much more reason, to rave and fantastiquize, as I doe, must necessarily be to doubt.'

But the Prince of Denmark cannot, like the country gentleman of Bordeaux, sleep soundly on a pillow of incuriosity, dismissing his doubts as bad dreams. Hamlet's pause, at the dead center of the play, is a prelude to 'action,' the last word in his soliloquy. That is the way in which conscience works in us all, he generalizes, albeit some of his critics have assumed that he is particularizing his own delay. Our spontaneous resolves are weakened by our intellectual compunctions; our will is puzzled before the unknowable. Having taken this long look, he will leap into a quick succession of adventures; he will make choices, right or wrong, thick and fast. The decisive event will be planned by others, and will play unexpectedly into his hands. Horatio will counsel last-minute hesitation, but Hamlet will be ready for anything. His final disjunction is a conditional syllogism: 'If it be now, 'tis not to come; if it be not to come, it will be now; if it be not now, yet it will come' (v.ii.231–4). Time will decide, and fate will thereafter seem to have been inevitable. Hamlet consoles himself with a reflection paraphrased from Montaigne: 'Since no man knows aught of what he leaves, what is't to leave betimes?' Another question which might be referred to the Ghost, since Hamlet's father seems to have known a good deal about what he left behind. By now that perturbed spirit must be at rest—which may or may not mean nonexistence. Nothing has been revealed about the undiscovered country, although the rottenness of Denmark has been laid bare. Like the nocturnal watchers on the platform before the castle, we are relieved when the cock crows, the apparition fades, and russet tinges the sky. In the half-light between knowledge and superstition, science and nescience, we can only be skeptical, neither affirming nor denying but doubting.

One of the most celebrated Hamlets of theatrical history,

Tommaso Salvini, summed up the part in a single trait: *il dubbio*. Hamlet is not so much a perplexing personality as he is a state of perplexity into which we enter, the very personification of doubtfulness. His sense of certainty has been fatally ravaged, and with it his trust in others. They are even less sure of things than he is; Polonius obliges him by discerning three different animals in the same cloud; and Osric agrees that the weather is hot or cold, depending upon Hamlet's variable taste. In the absence of some external criterion, he searches within. Whether this earth is a goodly frame or a sterile promontory, whether this air is fretted with golden fire or befouled with pestilent vapors, may depend on which of his two mental portraits we are able to keep in mind. Erasmus, borrowing an example from Plato, recalls those double images of Silenus, one of whose faces was antithetical to the other in every regard: '. . .what outwardly seemed death, yet loking within ye shulde fynde it lyfe: and on the other side, what semed life, to be death: what fayre, to be foule: what riche, beggerly: what cunnyng, rude: what stronge, feable: what noble, vile: what gladsome, sadde: what happie, unlucky: what friendly, unfriendly: what healthsome, noysome.' So Erasmus, in the English translation of the *Encomium Moriae* by Sir Thomas Chaloner, adds his testimonial to the conception of man as a two-faced biped. 'Briefely the Silene ones beyng undone and disclosed, ye shall fynde all thyngs tourned into a new semblance.' Whether that semblance is angelic or demonic, whether the mask indeed is tragic or comic, depends upon the attitude of the beholder.

'There is nothing either good or bad but thinking makes it so,' Hamlet explains to Rosencrantz and Guildenstern (II.ii.255–6). The identical situation, the state of Denmark, may seem good to them and bad to him. Similarly, an intellectual might have disagreed with a pair of courtiers about the state of England in 1601, though he could hardly have publicized his plaint. In the year of *Hamlet*, John Donne poured his disillusionment into an elaborate poetic fragment, 'The Progress of the Soul,' which breaks off with this triplet:

> Ther's nothing simply good, nor ill alone,
> Of every quality comparison,
> The only measure is, and judge, opinion.

Montaigne, under more tranquil circumstances two decades before, had reached an analogous position in an essay demonstrating 'That the taste of goods or evils doth greatly depend on the opinion we have of them.' Of these three formulations, Hamlet's is the boldest, though his boldness must be qualified by the realization that he is a fictitious character, speaking not for Shakespeare but for himself, and for himself in a particularly saturnine humor. Yet he is willing, at all events, to declare that there are no ethical absolutes, that good and evil are value-judgements determined by relative standards. Troilus, starting from the same relativism, strives to imbue it with all the enthusiasm that Hamlet so consciously lacks. 'What is aught save as 'tis valu'd?' asks Troilus. The upshot, for him, is a relentless devaluation of both the heroic and the romantic ideals. *Troilus and Cressida* has close affinities with *Hamlet* in composition and in temper; but it terminates with its difficulties unresolved. As for *Hamlet*, it never regains its lost certitudes; nor does it ever relax its movement of vacillation; but it derives new meaning out of its clash of values; and its overclouded patterns merge into a grander design. 'What doubt is to knowledge, irony is to the personal life,' wrote another melancholy Dane, Sören Kierkegaard, who was to strike his balance under the heading of *Either/Or*. That pronouncement asks for application, when Kierkegaard singles out Shakespeare as 'the grand master of irony.'

THE QUESTION OF HAMLET

III. IRONY

THE Gravedigger, who–like so many of Shakespeare's clowns–is an accomplished dialectician, explains to us that 'an act hath three branches–it is to act, to do, and to perform' (v.i.12–13). This is redundant logic, yet it serves a purpose; it rings the changes on a momentous word, and it comments obliquely on Hamlet's inaction. Moreover, lest we dally too long before his dilemmas, it reminds us that the argument must proceed to a third and decisive stage. Our thesis has been singular, in the person of a solitary being wholly surrounded by questions. Doubts, as to his relations with other beings, as to the basis of his continued existence, present themselves under the twofold aspect of an antithesis. These components must be resolved through a synthesis, pieced together out of the playwright's assumptions about the nature of human experience. The conventional five-act structure of tragedy is ignored by the Quartos of *Hamlet*, indicated for only the first two acts of the Folio text, and completed by later editors. Granville-Barker's recommendation, which best accords with modern theatrical usage, is that we conceive the play as a work composed in three movements. 'Treble woe' is the fatality that overtakes Polonius and his two children. Threefold also are the consequences of the original sin against the old King, his loss 'Of life, of crown, of queen' (I.v.75). The drama might almost be described as a triangle-play with a vengeance. The interrelationship of Hamlet the Elder, Claudius, and Gertrude predominates in the mind of Hamlet the Younger. Perhaps it has some bearing upon his tendency to triple his phrases: 'O, horrible! O, horrible! most horrible!' (I.v.80) 'Words, words, words' (II.ii.194). 'Mother, mother, mother!' (III.iv.6).

Our third trope, *ironia*, is more than a figure of speech or even of thought; it may be a point of view, a view of life, and—as such—a resolvent for contrarieties. Its most clear-cut form, designated in Puttenham's *Arte of English Poesie* as 'the drye mock,' is a statement which means the contrary of what it purports to say. Caesar was ambitious; Brutus was honorable; yet Antony contrives, by his mocking inflection, to carry the opposite impression in both regards. Dubious statements could be reversed by simply adding the Elizabethan interjection *quotha*. Hamlet makes the controversion explicit, when his mother asks him, 'What shall I do?' (III.iv.180). He has just told her, directly, 'go not to my uncle's bed.' Now he elaborates, 'Not this, by no means, that I bid you do.' In other words, what follows is to be taken ironically: 'Let the bloat King tempt you again to bed...' And Hamlet dwells, with ambivalent detail, on the endearments he would have her avoid. Given the hypocrisy of the court, where one may not say what one means, honesty must either hold its tongue or express itself through indirection. When Polonius begs to take his leave, Hamlet's tone of politeness thinly disguises his eagerness to confer the favor begged: 'You cannot, sir, take from me anything that I will more willingly part withal—' Whereupon his dry mock deepens into a thrice-uttered heartcry: 'except my life, except my life, except my life' (II.ii.217–21). To the initial queries of Claudius and Gertrude, his hedging answers are verbal ironies. Gertrude's naïve reaction to the Play-Queen—'The lady doth protest too much, methinks'—unconsciously lays bare her own standards of conduct. Hamlet's double-edged comment, 'O, but she'll keep her word,' is ostensibly another bit of polite conversation (III.ii.240–41).

Actually, he is distorting the play-within-the-play in order to drive home an invidious contrast. The Play-Queen will have no chance to keep her word; the Queen of Denmark had a chance and failed.

As for the King, his usual mode is merely hypocritical; but, under the goading of Hamlet, he too waxes ironic. When he announces the excursion to England, and Hamlet assents with 'Good,' Claudius says, 'So is it, if thou knew'st our purposes' (IV.iii.48–9). He is having his grim little joke, and assuming Hamlet is unaware that what might be good for Claudius would not be good for himself. But the joke is on Claudius; for he does not know that Hamlet knows his purposes, that he himself is rather a step behind than a step ahead of his opponent. Hamlet's retort is enigmatic, if not ironic, with its cryptic allusion to the Ghost: 'I see a cherub that sees them.' The irony now lies not in the statement but in the situation, which will turn out to be the contrary of what Claudius designs. Hamlet has already ventured a prediction, in his farewell to his mother. There, in hinting at the treachery of Rosencrantz and Guildenstern, whom he will trust as would 'adders fang'd,' he has defined the process of dramatic irony:

> For 'tis the sport to have the engineer
> Hoist with his own petar. (III.iv.203, 206–7)

It is always exciting when craft meets equal craftiness in a battle of wits. But there is peculiar satisfaction in watching, when vaunted cleverness overreaches itself. The comic formula of the cheater cheated, *Wily Beguiled*, is transmuted into the imagery of siege and explosion, as Hamlet conspires with himself to blow his enemies at the moon. The actual conspiracy, when it happens, will be literary rather than military; it will consist of forging a royal mandate, so that Rosencrantz and Guildenstern will be executed in Hamlet's place; and this will be retrospectively disclosed by Hamlet to Horatio, with rhetorical flourishes parodying the style of Claudius. Thus the episode has been somewhat glossed over, particularly the incidental deaths of the schoolfellows; but it had been a conspicuous feature of the primitive legend; and its elements, widely diffused in folklore, persist through the *motif* of a lucky youth with an ill-fated letter. Hamlet's prototype is the unsuspecting hero, sent on a journey bearing his own death-warrant; jolted into some realization of the hazards confronting him, he finally turns adversity into advantage.

Another element in the archaic tale has proved susceptible of endless refinement. This was the spectacle of a cunning hero forced to wear a mask of stupidity, which originally lent Hamlet his oafish name. In dissembling, in counterfeiting madness, in playing his antic part, he exemplifies the humanistic tradition of the wise fool. In his wayward fashion, he pursues the wisdom of Socrates, which characteristically masqueraded as ignorance. Hamlet's behavior has been characterized by a student of Shakespeare's wit and humor, John Weiss, as a 'sustained gesture of irony.' It is that gesture which enables the questioner to reject seeming for being, which helps the doubter to distinguish between appearance and reality. In the dual role of an ironist, Hamlet can remain his tragic self while presenting a quasi-comic front. The dissembler of Aristophanic comedy, the *eiron*, had shrewdly exposed the impostor or *alazon*. Neoclassicists like Voltaire were historically warranted in associating the ironic with the comic and deeming it inappropriate for tragedy. The concept was broadly extended by Bishop Thirlwall's essay 'On the Irony of Sophocles.' If the Greek tragedians had been ironists, it was not because they mocked at their fellow men, but because they concerned themselves with the mockery of fate. Oedipus is the engineer of his own downfall; and his blinding is a requital for taunting the blind Tiresias, as well as an expiation of his trespasses. Human agency seems to confound itself through the workings of some cosmic design. So it seems to the Play-King:

> Our wills and fates do so contrary run
> That our devices still are overthrown. (III.ii.221–2)

That overthrow is made ironic by the perception of counter-devices, by the aptness with which fates are matched against wills. The outcome must belie the expectation, the disappointment must become concrete, through some logical connection or personal association. This correspondence between device and counter-device takes its most obvious form in the equivocal oracle. The riddling prophecies that cajole and betray Macbeth are the merest plays upon words, which are carried out by charades on the part of Birnam Wood and Macduff. In *King Lear* the irony is classical when the gods are said to have justly taken Cornwall's life for Gloucester's sight; it is more problematic when Gloucester accuses them of treating mortals as wanton boys treat flies. Poetic justice, which prevails in *Macbeth*, miscarries in *King Lear*, where the ways of providence are as unfathomable as in *Hamlet*.

With *Hamlet*, as we have seen, we are involved in two sets of complementary problems. One set is speculative: why? wherefore? who is the Ghost? and what is the ultimate mystery that it prefigures? The other is practical: what shall we do? how should Hamlet bear himself amid these unexampled difficulties? and how should he accomplish his unsought vocation, revenge? Shakespearean tragedy is deeply concerned with the individual as he faces opportunity, responsibility, and moral choice. It is equally preoccupied with the pattern of events, and whether this is determined by casual accident, fatal necessity, or divine intervention. Given the motive, one must await one's cue. The interplay between these preoccupations is the source of innumerable ironies, both conscious and unconscious, some of them attached to the hero's viewpoint, others detached in a reminiscent overview. 'Hamlet has no plan, but *Hamlet* has,' as Goethe observed, with a fellow-dramatist's understanding. The play has a plot; and, so, in another sense, has the Prince; but he cannot foresee the fulfilment of his intentions; he can only test them against hugger-mugger conditions. Yet, as producer of 'The Murder of Gonzago,' he can take charge of a miniature drama which exerts an effect on the drama at large; he can play god and look down on his creation, in the self-conscious mood of romantic irony. Whereas in *Hamlet* itself, he is no more than a leading actor, whose body will be placed 'on a stage'—on a funeral bier which may likewise be viewed as a theatrical platform—among the other corpses at the end. It will then become Horatio's function to play the commentator, and to report upon the ironic upshot of the whole story: 'purposes mistook / Fall'n on th'inventors heads' (v.ii.389, 395–6).

Hamlet points the analogy himself when he addresses the surviving onlookers as 'audience to this act' (346). The verb 'to act' is synonymous with 'to do,' in the patient explanation of the Gravedigger, but also with the ambiguous 'to perform.' 'The name of action' has further branches for Hamlet; it often takes on this theatrical inflection, as when he declares that the customs of mourning are 'actions that a man might play' (I.ii.84). Conversely, he is pleading for sincerity, when he tells the Players: 'Suit the action to the word, the word to the action' (III.ii.19–20). The noun 'act' conveys a sexual innuendo, when it is bandied back and forth between Hamlet and Gertrude in the Closet Scene. Some of these ambiguities might be clarified in the light of God's law, if not of man's; for above us 'the action lies / In his true nature,' as Claudius confesses to himself (III.iii.61–2). Here below, deeds may be obfuscated by words, as they have been in his own case; or else they may be retarded by thoughts, as they are in Hamlet's.

> I do not know
> Why yet I live to say 'This thing's to do,'
> Sith I have cause, and will, and strength, and means
> To do't. (IV.iv.43–6)

Again and again he reproaches himself in this tone; but self-reproach is a sign of conscientiousness rather than cowardice. The Ghost reappears, at an awkward moment, to whet Hamlet's 'almost blunted purpose'; but ghosts, after all, are notorious for nagging, especially on the Elizabethan stage (III.iv.111). It takes no less than five of them to rouse Chapman's Senecal hero to *The Revenge of Bussy D'Ambois;* and yet his bravery is widely and loudly attested. Because we are privileged to overhear Hamlet's moments of self-questioning, or to glimpse his incertitude before psychic phenomena, we should not make the mistake of considering him a weak or passive figure. That his native disposition is active and resolute, though it has been temporarily sicklied over with the pale cast of melancholy—such an impression is fully confirmed by objective testimony from the other characters. '*Hamlet* is not a drama of weakness,' its Russian translator, Boris Pasternak, has clairvoyantly noted, 'but of duty and self-denial.'

The critical sentimentalization of Hamlet's personality has leaned heavily on the expression, *Gedankenschauspiel*, wrenched from its context in A. W. Schlegel's lectures and mistranslated as 'tragedy of thought.' This has encouraged the obscurantist conclusion that thought is Hamlet's tragedy; Hamlet is the man who thinks too much, ineffectual because he is intellectual; his nemesis is a failure of nerve, a nervous prostration. Schlegel wanted merely to underline the well-taken point that *Hamlet* was, above all, a drama of ideas, a dramatization of man's intellectual curiosity. By the canons of the humanists, the highest virtue was knowledge put into action. But how to know what to do? That was the question; there was the rub. Hamlet's plight is magnified by the tension between the stream of his highly skeptical consciousness and the undercurrents of murky superstition and swirling paganism. Hence he stands as the very archetype of character at odds with destiny, of the incompatibility between will and fate. He is a virtual prisoner, figuratively straining at gyves and fetters, yet capable of breaking away from 'the mutines in the bilboes' (v.ii.6). When he complains, 'I lack advancement,' Rosencrantz assumes that he is anxious for promotion; more likely, he is impatient to get on with his revenge (III.ii.354). 'The time is out of joint,' he sighs, as romantics and sentimentalists have sighed after him. But, though he curses the circumstance of his birth, he accepts his mission:

> O cursed spite
> That ever I was born to set it right. (I.v.189–90)

A similar tag, concluding the next act, marks his advance toward a plan:

> The play's the thing
> Wherein I'll catch the conscience of the King. (II.ii.632–3).

Hamlet's progress through the acts is marked by a sequence of such broken couplets, which seem to evoke an answering rhythm in the diction of Claudius:

> O come away!
> My soul is full of discord and dismay! (IV.i.44–5)

While Claudius seems to falter, Hamlet's threats become firmer, until he terminates his last soliloquy with a decision which moves from thought to action:

> . . . from this time forth
> My thoughts be bloody, or be nothing worth! (IV.iv.65–6)

Hamlet begins with a scholar's request to resume his studies at the university. He ends by being given a soldier's funeral. He is drawn into a psychological conflict: 'Sir, in my heart there was a kind of fighting. . .' (V.ii.4). This *agon* gradually leads to physical struggles, accompanied by vivid metaphors of reconnoitering spies and deploying battalions. His first maneuver is a strategic retreat, pursued by his antagonist's followers, who do not succeed in flushing him out. Then, as occasion will have it, he presses the Players into his service, and succeeds in outmaneuvering Claudius. Our attention shifts to the King with his first aside, which reveals to us that he has a conscience to be caught: 'O heavy burthen!' (III.i.54). Without this confession, we should not be certain of his guilt, and the play-within-the-play would lack its dimension of irony. What interests us, along with Hamlet and Horatio, is not the melodrama on the court stage but the psychodrama in Claudius' mind. 'This play is the image of a murther done in Vienna'—not at Elsinore (III.ii.247–8). The name of the duke's wife is Baptista, not Gertrude. No one would remember the late King, anyway; like the hobby-horse, he is forgotten. Any resemblances to real people or local situations are—or are they?—purely coincidental. 'The players cannot keep counsel,' says Hamlet, acting as prologue to the prologue, 'they'll tell all' (151–2). They will lodge the accusation that he has kept to himself, and we shall see if Claudius can keep counsel. Though their rhymes are stiff and didactic, they echo Hamlet's obsessions. One of his bitterest ironies was to attribute the haste of Gertrude's remarriage to palace economy, since it permitted the leftovers from the wake to be served at the wedding. 'Thrift, thrift, Horatio!' (I.ii. 180) This becomes a matter of principle in the Play-Queen's protestations:

> The instances that second marriage move
> Are base respects of thrift, but not of love. (III.ii.192–3)

To the Players Hamlet has expressed his distaste for 'inexplicable dumb shows' (III.ii.11). The pantomime that precedes and anticipates 'The Murder of Gonzago' is all too explicable; since we are not to see the whole of the play, it shows us what we shall miss. Yet Hamlet's presentation of something like his father's murder has been too emphatically straightforward for some of Shakespeare's critics, notably Dover Wilson, who has argued that the King must somehow have missed the dumb show in order to be able to sit through the ensuing production as long as he does. Mr. Wilson's hyper-ingenious interpretation seems to rest on the simple-minded postulate that, if Claudius witnessed the miming of his misdeed, he would react at once with reflexive alacrity. But, though he is guilty, Claudius is a hardened character, skilled at hiding his feelings and nearly able to brazen out Hamlet's test. Therein, to be precise, the scene derives its dramatic suspense: a murderer is being put through the third degree, and we are waiting and watching for signs of the psychological impact. These are not altogether wanting; as long as the actors are silent, so is Claudius; but when deeds are articulated by words, he voices his uneasiness with the suspicion that the play may contain offensive material; and it is under the cumulative ordeal that he breaks down, calls for lights, and stops the performance. The crucial business is the poisoning, together with the incantation of the poisoner, Lucianus. Now Lucianus is not Gonzago's brother; as Hamlet takes pains to point out, he is 'nephew to the King' (254). It follows, by implication, that what we have witnessed was not so much a re-enactment of King Hamlet's death as it was a preview of young Hamlet's revenge. The conscience of Claudius is trapped by fear for his life, as well as by remorse for his offence.

If the cap fits, Hamlet has taunted Claudius, put it on. 'Let the gall'd jade winch; our withers are unwrung' (252). At the top of his bent, amid the abrupt confusion that closes the Play

Scene, he versifies that sentiment: 'Why, let the stricken deer go weep, / The hart ungalled play. . .' The huntsman has hit his mark, and the beast has been caught napping. 'For some must watch, while some must sleep. . .' (282–4). The symbolic torches, hastily summoned, have cast their flickering light into dark corners. It is an exorcism, not of the honest ghost, but of the courtly dishonesty that obscures more sinister creatures, now 'frighted with false fire' (277). The comedy of masks is over, at all events; Hamlet has unmasked Claudius, revealing the inward villain behind the exterior smile. For the first time, Hamlet is sure of his object and free to act. His failure to do so, in the Prayer Scene, is a baffling mixture of coincidence and compunction, where fate tempts and will is puzzled. Here, it may seem in retrospect, Hamlet found the right moment and took the wrong turn. But would it have been better to plunge his rapier into the back of that proud man upon his knees at the *prie-dieu?* Claudius would live to say, 'No place indeed should murther sanctuarize' (IV.vii.128). Ironically, he would not realize that his own life had been spared through this momentary impulse of piety. Still more ironically, as he realizes, he has only been going through pious motions. He has desperately tried to pray, but he is too unregenerate a hypocrite: 'Words without thoughts never to heaven go' (III.iii.98). Meanwhile, his soliloquy has been crossed, so to speak, by Hamlet's; and Hamlet has decided to put up his sword, on the erroneous assumption that Claudius is purging his soul. Since Claudius does not succeed in repenting, Hamlet is retroactively deprived of his single reason for delay.

These cross-purposes were summed up in the word 'purgation,' when Rosencrantz and Guildenstern announced the King's indisposition after the play (III.ii.317). That purge has two double meanings, one physical and the other spiritual: blood-letting in a medical and in a homicidal sense, and purification through penance or through purgatory. Having brought to a stalemate the only scene in which he is alone with his arch-enemy, Hamlet plunges on to his mother's closet, where he makes the mistake of not hesitating. Slashing through the arras, he kills whoever is lurking there, presumably the King. It turns out to be Polonius, master of indirections, whose machination has reaped its reward by springing a final trap on himself. Consequently, Hamlet must withdraw for an interval, which is concentrated upon the two victims of the underplot: Laertes, forced to become his father's revenger; Ophelia, driven to madness and to death by water. Whether or not to accept the verdict of suicide is a doubtful question which we may leave to the Gravediggers. It is significant that Polonius, in rendering his mistaken diagnosis of Hamlet, blundered into a correct prognosis for his daughter. Hamlet's malady, he averred, was 'the very ecstasy of love,' to be feared because its violence 'foredoes itself' (II.i.102–3). The verb is prognostic; for Hamlet, as an unknown and unknowing spectator, will notice that the funeral rites are 'maimed' because the corpse 'did with desp'rate hand / Foredo it own life' (V.1.241–4). It is he who entertains the idea of self-slaughter; but it is the defenseless Ophelia whom the sea of troubles overwhelms. It is she who pronounces him insane, his noble mind overthrown, 'Like sweet bells jangled, out of tune and harsh' (III.i.166). But it is she who truly loses her mind, and drowns while singing 'snatches of old tunes' (IV.vii.179).

Imagery functions as a guide to Shakespeare's irony. Reason, like the music of the spheres, is a harmonious ideal; mental breakdown, transposed into sound, should be discordant; yet Ophelia, with her off-key ballads, turns 'affliction' into 'prettiness,' discord into harmony (IV.V.187–8). Gertrude, lyrically recounting Ophelia's 'muddy death,' emphasizes her 'melodious lay' (IV.vii.188–9). Gertrude's elegy also draws on that floral symbolism which Ophelia poignantly invoked on her round of farewells, and which has wreathed her in a special fragrance from her first scene to her burial. Laertes, warning her that Hamlet's affection may be 'sweet' but 'not lasting,' has compared it to 'A violet in the youth of primy nature' (I.iii.7–8). To his forbidding 'No more,' she responds with a gentle tremor: 'No more but so?' Whereupon he repeats his rigid denial: 'Think it no more.' In the Graveyard Scene, the same language and meter re-echo when Laertes asks, 'Must there no more be done?'. And the Priest replies with the sepulchral refrain, 'No more be done' (v.i.257). Whereupon Laertes cries,

> Lay her i' th' earth;
> And from her fair and unpolluted flesh
> May violets spring! (261–3)

Like the adverb 'nevermore,' so indelibly associated with the death of a beautiful young woman by Edgar Allan Poe, the hopeless phrase 'no more' runs through the play. It figures meaningfully in Hamlet's soliloquies: 'To die—to sleep— / No more. . . .', 'A beast, no more.' It is repeated three times by the Queen in her effort to stave off Hamlet's reprimand (III.iv.88, 94, 101). Gertrude, again, takes up the theme of flowers in strewing Ophelia's grave—not with 'dust to dust' but with 'Sweets to the sweet!' (v.i.266). The harsh priest believes that Ophelia should have stones instead of her 'virgin crants' or maiden garland; she should have been buried in unhallowed ground, without any ceremony whatever. She has been most distressed by the unceremonious interment accorded to her ceremonious father. She has even modified one of her songs to make it clear that flowers were omitted; since that day, the violets have all withered (IV.v.38, 185). In lamenting Hamlet's distraction, she evoked another flower, a Tudor emblem, 'Th' expectancy and rose of the fair state' (III.i.160). When her brother first beholds her in her distraught condition, he exclaims, 'O rose of May!' (IV.v.157).

Laertes, who has departed for Paris under somewhat Chesterfieldian auspices, returns to Elsinore as a very angry young man, breaking through the palace guard with a threat of political rebellion, and jumping into Ophelia's grave with a gesture of histrionic rivalry. Hamlet, as the destined object of his revenge, well understands that Laertes is behaving like a revenger. Hamlet's mirror-like intelligence, from first to last, is sensitive to such examples. All occasions seem to offer models for him to emulate: the Player brings out emotions which he must otherwise keep to himself; the soldier, personified by Fortinbras, sets an example as a man of action. His faithful friend, Horatio, on the other hand, is the type of man who could suffer misfortune without becoming the slave of passion. In this respect, Horatio's independence is contrasted with the sponginess of Rosencrantz and Guildenstern. However, the greatest exemplar is Hamlet's dead father, a precedent no living man could adequately parallel, least of all his successor, Claudius. This we have recognized as the central antithesis of the many that lend the play its structure, such as that between Gertrude and Ophelia. But, since the Ghost must act through the Prince, the effectual opposition is between Claudius and Hamlet himself; and, since Hamlet starts by regarding Claudius as his father's rival, his ability to take up the quarrel is the measure of his own growth toward maturity. He will not admit, to Rosencrantz and Guildenstern, that he hoped to inherit the crown; or that, more exactly, as heir presumptive, he hoped to be elected King. Yet to the Queen he speaks of Claudius as 'a cutpurse of the empire' who has stolen 'the precious diadem' (III.iv.99–100). And to Horatio, under the seal of confidence, he does admit that this opportunistic adventurer has 'Popp'd in between th'election and my hopes' (v.ii.65).

Claudius, on his side, is wary enough to regard Hamlet as a potential rival. He does not seem uneasy about his throne; he behaves with courage and dignity when Laertes enters with the mob; he even dares, somewhat ambiguously, to claim the divine right of kings. His wariness in dealing with Hamlet is grounded, partly on his love for Gertrude and Gertrude's love for her son, but largely on his calculation that Hamlet is popular (IV.vii.18). 'He's lov'd of the distracted multitude,' and Claudius' observation of that fact is couched in terms that reflect his own unpopularity (IV.iii.4). The people seem to be in favor of Hamlet, howbeit the courtiers are at the disposal of Claudius. Rosencrantz and Guildenstern devote a pair of their flattering speeches to the dependence of the subject upon the well-being of the monarch (III.iii.11–23). They could hardly expect to be giving their lives so soon in the royal service; yet their over-eagerness is Hamlet's excuse for the counter-trick by which he saves himself and pays them off. They asked for it: 'Why, man, they did make love to this employment!' (v.ii.57). In the duel of nerves between the two major antagonists, the Prince and the King, 'Between the pass and fell incensed points / Of mighty opposites,' these are minor casualties–like the deaths of Polonius, Laertes, Ophelia, and Gertrude. Hamlet virtually has to fight his way across their corpses, in coming to grips with his foe. The latter, securely entrenched and well attended by sycophants, holds the advantages in the struggle for power. The former must conquer more than his own repugnance; he must overcome the natural obstacles and the tactical diversions that impede him from his objective.

Hamlet is certainly planless when he allows himself to be exiled. The burden of his parting soliloquy is that the 'event,' the result of any difficult course of action, must be 'invisible,' unforseeable to the participant beforehand (IV.iv.50). Therefore it cannot be calculated too precisely in advance; one must take one's chances, like Fortinbras. The off-stage voyage, heading for England, brings the story home to Shakespeare's audience; but fortune intervenes upon the high seas; and Hamlet's most heroic adventures must be relayed by narrative. He is spared the embarrassment of talking about his own prowess through the letter read by Horatio, describing the encounter with the pirates to which Hamlet owed his release. That emergency is quite fortuitous, and he meets it like a true Viking. Not only does he act, but he acts more vigorously than his shipmates; he alone, in his instant of 'compelled valour,' boards the pirate ship and—by literally taking things into his own hands—makes the misadventure his turning-point (IV.vi.15). The Hamlet that emerges to dominate the Fifth Act is a new man who, like the heroes of epic, has attained his full stature during a strenuous interlude of exile and return. No longer need he eat the chameleon's dish or feel rebuked by the example of others. He has achieved a sense of his own identity, and he proclaims it from Ophelia's grave: 'This is I, / Hamlet the Dane.' (V.i.280–81). In the same breath he declares his love for her to the world and takes upon himself his father's title, the kingly epithet usurped by Claudius. Later Hamlet tells Horatio how he imprinted the 'Danish seal' on the forged mandate, utilizing his 'father's signet' (V.ii.49–50). It was the act of a king.

Hamlet's letter to Claudius, announcing his rearrival, is a challenge as well as a piece of bad news. Nonetheless the King adapts himself to the change, with his customary cleverness, by tarring on the unappeased Laertes. In the duel of mighty opposites, Claudius is represented by deputies, who defend him by parrying Hamlet's thrusts. Of these, Laertes, who has public support for the kingship, is the last and the most formidable. Hamlet does not think of him as a model, although, when the contest between them is proposed, he outdoes Osric in the extravagance of his praise: 'to make true diction of [Laertes], his semblable is his mirror, and who else would trace him, his umbrage, nothing more' (v.ii.123–5). Claudius, on the other side, fans the flames of competition, by falsely reporting that Hamlet is envious of Laertes' chivalric accomplishments. Flattery is reinforced by a testimonial from another man of parts, a gentleman of Normandy, so skilled in horsemanship that he has seemed 'incorps'd and deminatur'd / With the brave beast' (IV.vii.88–9). Claudius digresses to such an extent, in citing this shadowy witness, that we may wonder what ulterior purpose he–or Shakespeare–had in introducing him. Do we perceive, in the centaur-like description, another emblem of man in his animal guise? Or may we take a hint from the Quarto reading, where the Frenchman's name–Lamound in the Folio–is spelled Lamord? Could that have been, by an easily possible slip of typography or pronunciation, La Mort? And could that equestrian stranger be a premonitory vision of Death on a pale horse, heralding the outcome of the duel? That vision appears unexpectedly in familiar places; in the squares of Paris, as Rilke imagined them, Madame Lamort, the fateful dressmaker, winds and binds the restless ways of the world.

The physical altercation between Hamlet and Laertes, after being pacified by the mourners in the graveyard, is resumed on the artificial plane of a courtly tournament. The mannerisms of Osric re-establish an atmosphere in which 'The phrase' is much too elaborate to be 'germane to the matter' (v.ii.165). But this can no longer be taken seriously; Hamlet has definitively put aside the embittered sarcasm of his antic manner; and he fences with Osric in the verbiage of the affected courtier. The wager, to which he assents, is the irony of ironies: that, after all their mutual animosity, he should be the King's champion and fight on behalf of Claudius! Laertes seems likely to win, in spite of the odds; and Claudius would cheerfully lose six Barbary horses to be safely rid of his nephew. In his apology, which repudiates his madness, Hamlet is not able to deny it; but his blank verse is once again the idiom of his sanity, and of a touching sincerity when he speaks of misdirecting an arrow and wounding his brother. Laertes' response, dictated by the guile of Claudius, rings uncharacteristically false; he is not yet 'satisfied in nature,' though he pretends to be; and, as for 'honour,' what has that to do with the villainy he is about to perpetrate? (255,257). Claudius, in his falsified account of Hamlet's envy, used the metaphorical verb 'envenom,' and then went on to suggest that Laertes requite his adversary by using an unblunted sword (IV.vii.104). Laertes, in accepting this suggestion, added a Machiavellian touch of his own, that the sword's point be dipped in literal venom. He has already procured the poison, or 'unction,' and his ambiguous term reminds us of the poisoned King and the sacrament he had missed. The retribution will be a general poisoning, with short shrift for the present King, his Queen, and both of the champions.

Hamlet, not knowing what is in store for him this time, undertakes in sport what his partner has plotted in earnest. 'I'll be your foil, Laertes,' he volunteers, graciously implying that his inexperience will set off his opponent's dexterity (V.ii.266). When foils of another kind are brought in, as Claudius predicted, Hamlet is too high-minded to note that one of them—the one Laertes selects—is sharp and envenomed. Laertes is somewhat troubled by his conscience, as we gather from an aside; and Hamlet accuses him of holding back when, to the increasing consternation of Claudius, the Prince has won the first and second passes. Hence the third is the critical bout; the tainted weapon changes hands in the shuffle; and each of the swordsmen fatally wounds the other. Claudius could hardly have envisaged such a reprisal, when he incited Laertes to dispatch Hamlet 'with a little shuffling' (IV.vii.138). Looking momentarily toward heaven, Claudius had soliloquized: 'There is no shuffling' (III.iii.61). There our acts cannot be cancelled; there offence is revealed and punished; while here, on earth, we frequently manage to circumvent justice. Yet justice triumphs when Laertes is slain by his own rapier, as he acknowledges. Osric asks him how he feels, and he replies: 'Why, as a woodcock to mine own springe, Osric' (v.ii.317). His ending harks back to his father's early suspicions: 'Ay, springes to catch woodcocks!' (I.iii.115). Hamlet's vows to Ophelia were no more than traps for foolish birds, to the cautious Polonius. The old councillor, who saw springes everywhere, was grievously ensnared himself by one of them. Laertes, beginning with sage advice to his sister, does not heed her counter-warning. Neither the father nor the son has recked his own rede.

Shakespeare has a way of tagging his ironies through the use of images relating an earlier statement to a changed situation. The present image also relates the underplot, the self-sought ensnarement of Polonius and his family, to the main plot, the trapping of Claudius. But there is one more incidental victim, the fickle matriarch who comes between her son and husband once too frequently. Just as Hamlet has slain Polonius while intending to slay Claudius, so Claudius poisons Gertrude with a drink intended for Hamlet. Claudius himself is a hard drinker, much to the disdain of his temperate nephew. He seems to have a Scandinavian fondness for turning a celebration into a carousal, as he did after the Council Scene, calling for a cannonade with every royal toast. Now again wine is provided, healths are hypocritically drunk, and Hamlet's hits are saluted by the cannoneers on the battlements, so that every movement seems to have cosmic reverberations: "The cannons to the heavens, the heaven to earth' (v.ii.288). Into the trap he has been preparing for Hamlet, Claudius tosses one last bit of bait. Into Hamlet's cup he drops a 'union,' a large and flawless pearl, which—he significantly adds—is 'Richer than that which four successive kings / In Denmark's crown have worn' (284–5). Claudius is tantalized when Hamlet delays his potation, after winning his first two exchanges, and silently tortured when Gertrude sips from 'the poison'd cup' (303). When the stricken Laertes confesses, Hamlet turns his lethal sword against the chief plotter and sedentary duelist. At long last, the protagonist has the antagonist in his power. But Claudius is tough, and Hamlet makes sure by forcing the cup to his lips. Union, quotha! The ironic image is now a symbolic pun. The pearl is indeed a reward for Hamlet, symbolizing the violent termination of Gertrude's marriage:

> Here, thou incestuous, murd'rous, damned Dane,
> Drink off this potion! Is thy union here?
> Follow my mother. (336–8)

If Claudius is united in death with Gertrude, Hamlet will be following them both in another moment—and what, then, of the Ghost? Is it fully at rest? has it returned to the undiscovered country? and was it a spirit of health or a goblin damned, after all? we still may ask, as we contemplate the carnage. The ghost of the murdered warrior, in *The Spanish Tragedy*, presides at the catastrophe of that play, and promises to usher the ghosts of the other characters to their proper punishments in the next world. But Shakespeare knew that tragedy is diminished, when the harshest fact of experience is softened by sentimental myths of the afterlife. Hamlet's last words, before he enters the silence from which he has previously recoiled, are as rigorous as the final proposition in the *Tractatus Logico-Philosophicus:* 'Whereof one cannot speak, thereof one must be silent.' Shakespeare has spoken much about death in this play and elsewhere, but always about our apprehension of it, and usually to intensify our appreciation of life. 'To die' is neither to sleep nor to dream, for Claudio in *Measure for Measure;* it is to 'go we know not where.' Claudio, much more ardently than Hamlet, would rather bear the worst ills of this life than escape to others which might prove worse. The decomposition of the body, in Claudio's harrowing speech, is a certainty; the torments in store for the soul are possibilities imagined by 'lawless and incertain thought.' For Hamlet, welcoming death when it comes unsought, felicity seems to loom ahead in the prospect of nonexistence rather than the relish of salvation, in shuffling off mortal coils which have ceased to be bearable. But his *alter ego* may not commit suicide; Horatio still has painful obligations to fulfil 'in this harsh world' (359).

Since life continues despite the inroads of death, order must be restored at the Danish court and certain clarifications must be made public. As the play concludes on the level of the over-plot, the waning *dramatis personae* are eked out by the convergence of the English embassy and the Norwegian army. The survival of Horatio is a guarantee of continuity, while the entrance of Fortinbras settles the issue of succession. Three claimants to the crown lie dead at his feet. Claudius had acquired it by murdering its rightful possessor, King Hamlet, thereby instigating the revenge of the Prince, his son. But Hamlet, in the course of that undertaking, had stumbled into the slaughter of Polonius, which his son, Laertes, was thereupon provoked into revenging against Hamlet himself. Each of these revengers kills the other, although Hamlet lives long enough to kill Claudius, and Laertes to say, 'He is justly serv'd,' before the two 'Exchange forgiveness' and die (338, 340). But there has been another revenge afoot, the very first we heard about in the play, amid the rumors of preparation for war. This was the expedition of young Fortinbras against Denmark, in retaliation for King Hamlet's victory and the slaying of his father, King Fortinbras. Through the diplomacy of Voltemand and Cornelius, Norway has been persuaded to divert its warlike energies toward that perennial scapegoat of European imperialism, Poland. On this errand, Fortinbras' path has crossed Hamlet's, and Hamlet has admired his resolution. Now he reappears victorious, and Hamlet's 'dying voice' has assured him the throne (367). All that the old King fought for has been lost; his dynasty is extinct; his land will be ruled by the scion of his enemy. Fortinbras, an exemplary figure, having foregone his revenge, has inherited the kingdom. (See Figure 2, page 167).

Under the circumstances, can it be concluded that the disjointed state is back in frame, that the time has been set right? The wicked are destroyed; but so are the merely officious, and even the innocent. There is not much virtue to be rewarded; Hamlet seems to have been more virtuous while he resisted his vindicative mission. His resistance, as well as his own destruction, may be justified on the grounds that he who lives by the sword will perish by it. The legendary Hamlet lived to be crowned and to reign for many years, whereafter his happy ending had a sequel involving betrayal and further hostilities. To convey this perpetual insecurity, within the limits of the dramatic medium, Shakespeare kills off his hero prematurely. Yet, in the manner of their respective deaths, Hamlet and his opponents differ completely. None of them—Claudius, Laertes, Polonius, Rosencrantz, Guildenstern—is expecting to die. Neither is Gertrude; Ophelia, as usual, is the doubtful case. Whereas Hamlet has prepared himself by philosophizing, in the traditional sense that philosophy is learning how to die. He has also shown his bravery, from his first encounter with the Ghost: 'I do not set my life at a pin's fee' (I.iv.65). Nevertheless, he has held back; as he accuses himself in his final soliloquy, he has waited because he wanted to make sure of the event, forgetting that 'what is mortal and unsure' cannot determine the future for itself (IV.iv.51). Under the stress of exile, he has had to act rashly—'And prais'd be rashness for it.' The best that free will can do, he has discovered, is to 'rough-hew' our ends; the ultimate pattern must somehow be shaped by 'a divinity' (V.ii.10–11). Claudius, in an identical cadence, has recently placed his kingship under the protection of that unaccountable divinity (IV.v.123–5). He has been protected by his prayer, for better and worse, and by the bungled death of Polonius.

Hamlet, upon discovering the wrong body, began to realize that events were subject to ulterior causation, which had cast him both as punisher and as punished, divine agent and accursed instrument:

> ... heaven hath pleas'd it so,
> To punish me with this, and this with me,
> That I must be their scourge and minister. (III.iv.173–5)

Heaven is also 'ordinant' in Hamlet's liberation at the expense of Rosencrantz and Guildenstern, or so he feels; though he seems to have actively collaborated in their deaths, they are not on his conscience (V.ii.48). To understand how higher forces operate would be to profess the foreknowledge that he disclaims. 'We defy augury,' he confides to Horatio, 'there's a special providence in the fall of a sparrow' (V.ii.230–1). The illustration, borrowed from the Gospels, seems to avow a mystical belief in divine immanence. Yet Hamlet waxes increasingly fatalistic as he approaches the crisis, and the same speech culminates with one of his stoical echoes from Montaigne: '...what is't to leave betimes?' His speculative questions have been reduced to the practical question of timing: 'The readiness is all.' In *King Lear*, although the emphasis is transferred from youth to age and from acting to suffering, the moral runs succinctly parallel and is enunciated at a parallel phase of the drama: 'Ripeness is all.' After so much brooding upon things past, after so much guesswork about what is to come, Hamlet is wholly concentrated upon the immediacy of the present. 'If it be now, . . . if it be not now. . .' The recurring insistence on the monosyllable 'now' heightens the vivid sensations of life facing death, as it does in Ernest Hemingway's story of a dying writer, 'The Snows of Kilimanjaro.' Within a few minutes the arriving ambassadors, with their news that Claudius' scheme has miscarried, will precipitate Hamlet's arrest; and he is still without any scheme of his own. 'The interim is mine,' he boldly declares. 'And a man's life's no more than to say "one" '—no longer than the monosyllabic duration of the first thrust in the one-two-three of a duel.

That sententious remark has urgent concreteness, since there is one man's life which Hamlet must quickly deal with. The interim will be short; but it will put a rapier into his hand and bring him into the presence of Claudius. The duel itself must seem to promise no more than a harmless exercise. Hamlet has no animus against his challenger, as he assured him in the Graveyard Scene: 'But it is no matter' (v.i.313). To Horatio he repeats the same phrase, in brushing aside his own vague misgivings (v.ii.223). Nothing matters now, least of all his own life; if he completes his task, as he has resolved, he is out of irony's reach; whereas Claudius and Laertes are ready to be hoist by the trick they have engineered. Laertes' splenitive rashness is the foil that sets off Hamlet's thoughtsick hesitancy. Laertes has not paid much heed to his prudent father's advice: '. . . Nor any unproportion'd thought his act.' Above all, he has not been true to himself; he has been untrue to his brotherly nature in colluding with Claudius, and in tainting his sword with the poisonous unction. Hence it follows, as the night the day, that he is false to his friend; he, too, is his brother's murderer. When Osric praises Laertes, Hamlet qualifies his approval by saying, 'to know a man well were to know himself' (146). It is because Hamlet knows himself that he can be true to himself; self-knowledge is the precondition of the integrity that

Laertes crucially lacks; hence introspection is a source of strength rather than a weakness of Hamlet's character. André Gide has written, commenting on Montaigne, that the only indubitable knowledge is that of one's self. And Montaigne has cited the admonition of Cicero: '*This is the total summe of all, that you be master of your selfe.*'

Self-mastery may alternatively demand an exertion of will or a submission to fate. Circumstances are beyond our control, much more often than not; our best endeavor is to control ourselves, if we can. 'Lord, we know what we are,' Ophelia moans prophetically, 'but we know not what we may be' (IV.v.43). Hamlet, the scholar-prince, dies suddenly like a soldier-king on a battlefield, eulogized by the belligerent Fortinbras, and borne off the stage to a higher stage for a military funeral. This is the most striking of many contrasts, when we are invited to measure him beside his contemporary, Don Quixote, who retires in defeat to his study and to a lucid and peaceful deathbed. Until that belated hour of self-recognition, he has never doubted that he was born to set things right. Nor could he be accused of lacking a plan; whenever it miscarried, as it has invariably done, he has offered some sort of contingent excuse. But his rout and retirement have thoroughly demonstrated the impracticality of his project for combining the two professions of arms and letters. Thought, instead of guiding retarded action, has overleaped itself. The irony of Cervantes is based on the rhetorical device of *antiphrasis*—or, more concretely, on the mock-heroic disparity between the style and the subject. What happens to the hero is a joke to everyone except himself. What happens in *Hamlet* is a secret discernible to the hero alone. He knows what the others do not; the others know what Don Quixote does not. Hamlet, as *eiron*, exposes the high and mighty pretensions of the *alazon*, Claudius; and when the pretender falls, the whole superstructure of courtly appearances collapses with him. But Shakespeare, as the master ironist, is not content to undermine superficial ideals; his profounder concern is with the recognition of underlying realities.

Circumstantial irony, at its simplest, may be exemplified by Lucian's Charon, who laughs because he has seen a falling tile kill a man who has just accepted an invitation to dinner. The situation became more comprehensive, but scarcely more complex, when the Lisbon earthquake erupted to shatter Voltaire's optimistic faith in a rational cosmos, where everything was teleologically ordained for human convenience and comfort. Such encounters with sheer contingency may be as inevitable as they are unpredictable; and tragedy is at least a forewarning against them, a warning lest our blessings be turned into curses. Moreover, it is an attempt to indicate limits which we may overstep at our peril, to locate the point where our wills converge with our fates, to discern the odds that confront and confound our best-laid plans. Vengeance is its most habitual theme because the revenger is called upon to take into his own hands what might better be left to providence, however we define it; and if the revenge gets out of hand and goes amiss, as it is almost bound to do, if the mistaken purposes fall upon their inventors' heads, then that reversal is an ironic commentary upon the ways of human destiny. Since we cannot altogether arrange our lives, we are constantly seeking some principle of arrangement in the universe, whether it be the finger of deity or the determination of chance. Thwarted, we may blame fickle fortune with Seneca, or malicious fate with Thomas Hardy, or original sin with Kierkegaard. Otherwise, our quest for retribution, with Dante, must be continued in another world. Lesser dramatists are easily tempted to intervene in the little worlds they have created, making sure that the good have their rewards when the evil have their punishments; but insofar as they improve upon life, they weaken their dramaturgy.

With Shakespeare the dramatic resolution conveys us, beyond the man-made sphere of poetic justice, toward the ever-receding horizons of cosmic irony.

This is peculiarly the case with *Hamlet*, for the same reasons that it excites such intensive empathy from actors and readers, critics and writers alike. There may be other Shakespearean characters who are just as memorable, and other plots which are no less impressive; but nowhere else has the outlook of the individual in a dilemma been so profoundly realized; and a dilemma, by definition, is an all but unresolvable choice between evils. Rather than with calculation or casuistry, it should be met with the virtue of readiness; sooner or later it will have to be grasped by one or the other of its horns. These, in their broadest terms, have been—for Hamlet, as we interpret him—the problem of what to believe and the problem of how to act. Hamlet is unwittingly compelled to act as if life were a duel, with unbated swords and against a series of furtive assailants. He is unwillingly led to believe that death comes as a cup, filled with poisonous wine and containing a flawless pearl. His doom is generalized in Fulke Greville's chorus:

> Oh, wearisome condition of humanity,
> Born under one law, to another bound . . .

Irony cannot solve the incalculable contradictions between the personal life and the nature of things. Yet it can teach us to live with them; and that is no mean achievement; for Hamlet's knowledge was not idle reflection, according to Nietzsche. It was an insight which hindered action by stripping the veil of illusion from the terrible truth, the terror or the absurdity of existence. This would be intolerable, were it not for the transformations of art, which asserts man's conquest over his fears, and which thereby allays his vexation of spirit. Thus Hamlet's limited victory commences with the play-within-the-play, a working-model of the play itself, which repeats the lesson in mastery on a larger scale within our minds. From its very commencement, after the stroke of midnight, we are brought face to face with the supernatural. Volleys of gunfire augment and accelerate the sound effects until, at the conclusion of the dead-march, '*a peal of ordinance*' signalizes a battle lost and won.

Shortly after the First World War and not long before the Second, Paul Valéry imagined a ravaged Europe as a battlement paced by a latter-day Hamlet, apostrophizing the ghosts of many dead heroes. But the skull to which he addressed himself was not that of Yorick; it had belonged to Leonardo da Vinci, the artist-engineer who had dreamed of flying machines but not of bombing planes. That ironic fancy of Valéry's has been grimly multiplied by the supreme feats of destructive engineering accomplished during the generation that has passed since he wrote. Today we need no Horatio to expound the rumors of armament races or the reports of foreign negotiations. To watch the various petards explode, grossly enlarged as they have been by misdirected thought and unplanned action, is no longer anything like sport. Our consciences are caught in that bigger and better mousetrap which civilization has so proudly contrived and so cunningly baited for itself. Well may we call, like Claudius, for light. We too are guilty creatures at a play, and our withers have been feelingly wrung. Or rather, in Valéry's phrase, we are undergoing a crisis of the intellect. Up to a certain point, the modern mind has taken the course of Faust; it has felt free to experiment, to cultivate the widest experience, to develop and enrich personality. Past that point, it has been taking the way of Hamlet; it has been curbed and sidetracked, commandeered by unexpected emergencies and forced to expend itself on objects unworthy of its talents. But, happily, the parable does not end with our ephemeral efforts to apply it. It persists while thinking man is interested in viewing his finest self-portrait, in asking himself the reason for his existence, or in responding to those demands which may prove, in the long run, to be its justification.

SUPPLEMENTARY STUDIES

THE ANTIC DISPOSITION

To define true madness,
What is't but to be nothing else but mad?

HAmlet's state of mind is one of those questions upon which all the doctors have disagreed. Even professional alienists have offered their diagnoses; yet discussion has been no more conclusive, and definition no less redundant or circular, than the rhetorical question posed by Polonius (II.ii. 193–4). At one extreme the answer has been bounded by unequivocal statements in the sources that, as the English translation of Belleforest puts it, 'Hamblet counterfeited the madman.'[1] At the other it has been bemused by the assumption, which proved particularly congenial to romantic actors like Edwin Booth, that Hamlet was really the victim of the mental disease he claimed to be simulating; in other words, his pretence was pretended, a ruse of madman's cunning. Continental observers have diagnosed it as 'the first and greatest manifestation of the English malady, Spleen.'[2] Consultation with contemporaneous authorities on medicine and psychology has illuminated, if not solved, the problem.[3] Hamlet was suffering, so they inform us, from 'melancholy adust'—or, as we might say, having a nervous breakdown. The Elizabethan term, although it depends upon an outmoded physiological concept, is scarcely less precise than our modern expression. Both imply that Hamlet's case is not chronic, that since his father's death his conduct has been uncharacteristic, and that he is not his courtly, scholarly, soldierly self during the interval when we are his witnesses. Hamlet himself is quite explicit upon this point; and in his Third Soliloquy, the single occasion on which he refers to melancholy, he couples it with weakness (II.ii.629). That it is symptomatic of an underlying malaise, which has an objective and external cause, his sharpest observer, Claudius, is all too well aware:

> There's something in his soul
> O'er which his melancholy sits on brood. (III.i.172–3)

Something turns out to be nothing less than revenge, deeply motivated and deviously hatched. However, the motive for Hamlet's eccentric behavior is not that of his legendary prototype, whose father had been openly slain and whose own life would be directly threatened if he were not considered a harmless madman. Hamlet stands in need of a new *persona*, once the Ghost has excited his suspicions, not so much in order to feel his way as to speak his mind with impunity. 'Give thy thoughts no tongue' is the first commandment in the world of Polonius (I.iii.59). From the outset Hamlet feels constrained to hold his tongue, to keep his counsel in soliloquy (I.ii.159); with his fellow courtiers, as with the players, gradually he learns to 'show fairly outwards' (II.ii.391–2). The mere show of mourning, he has retorted to Gertrude, is far surpassed by the actuality of his grief. She had begun by asking him to 'cast thy nighted colour off' (I.ii.67). He will comply, with a vengeance, when he decides to 'put an antic disposition on' (I.v.172). Claudius will all but understand, in wondering 'why he puts on this confusion' (III.i.2); and Hamlet will employ the same verb, *put on*, in exhorting Gertrude to assume a virtue she may not possess (III.iv.160). Attributes and attitudes are habitually put on and taken off, as if they were clothes, in Shakespeare's imagery. In *1 Henry IV* the Prince serves notice that he will soon 'throw off' his 'loose behaviour' (I.ii.232). He too must play an assumed part, as Falstaff jocosely reminds him: 'Thou art essentially mad without seeming so' (II.iv.540–41). Hamlet reverses that outlook in a moment of hectic irony, by telling Gertrude to tell Claudius.

> That I essentially am not in madness,
> But mad in craft. (III.iv.187–8).

Madness, as the abandonment of reason, is a constant danger throughout the play, from Horatio's desperate warning against the Ghost (I.iv.69–74) through Hamlet's disingenuous apology to Laertes (v.ii.241–50). Yet Hamlet is clearly thoughtsick rather than brainsick—neurotic rather than psychotic, to state the matter in more clinical terms. In his battle of wits with Rosencrantz and Guildenstern, he is led to affirm that his 'wit's diseas'd' (III.ii.333); but he has already come closer to the mark in characterizing himself as 'mad north-north-west' (II.ii.397). He is, indeed, what circumstance has made him, a monomaniac. He can distinguish shrewdly enough between a hawk and a handsaw, or expatiate with lucidity and brilliance upon many another theme. But his obsession with his mother's marriage and his hostility against his uncle are forbidden themes which he may not harp on unless he is granted a certain license, not to say licentiousness. This 'crafty madness' provides him with a means of expressing pent-up emotions, which are communicated to the audience through asides and soliloquies, but which can find no release until they reach the other characters through a sequence of sharply pointed *contretemps*. Thus his denunciation of feminine frailty, though its appropriate target will be Gertrude, first falls upon the bewildered ears of the innocent Ophelia, who thereupon concludes that he is mad. His intelligence has never been keener than when he soliloquized a few moments before; while her pronouncement, 'O what a noble mind is here o'erthrown!', will reverberate ironically; for it is her reason which will be sacrificed, 'Like sweet bells jangled, out of tune and harsh' (III.i.158–66).

One way or another, it is not surprising that the play should have become a byword for preoccupation with insanity. Three of Shakespeare's contemporaries burlesqued it in *Eastward Ho*, where a footman named Hamlet calls for 'my lady's coach,' and is asked by a tankard-bearer: 'Are you mad?' (III.ii.4,6). Mallarmé recalls a production at a French provincial theater, which was billed as *Hamlet, ou le Distrait*.[4] A recent study of 'madness as a theatrical medium' dates its English popularity during the early years of the seventeenth century from Shakespeare's example.[5] In this respect, however, as in so many others, Shakespeare in turn was following the example of that most popular of all Elizabethan or Jacobean plays, *The Spanish Tragedy*, or *Hieronimo's Mad Again*. Kyd's subtitle suggests that interest centered upon the fits and remissions of the hero's lunacy. Shakespeare's first tragic hero, Titus Andronicus, crudely observes that precedent; though he is undoubtedly driven insane, he goes on having his lucid intervals, and 'his feigned ecstasies' as well (IV.iv.21). When, 'to feed his brainsick humours,' Tamora and her sons disguise themselves as personifications of Revenge, Murder, and Rapine, he recognizes her as Lear will recognize Gloucester: 'I know thee well enough' (V.ii.71,21). And Titus knows well enough how to complete the Senecan catastrophe by serving the sons to their mother baked in a pie. These formalities are duly matched by the rant and bombast of the style. All of *Titus Andronicus*, except for two brief scenes of intentional comedy, is written in the blank verse standardized by the Tragedy of Revenge.

Here again, the pattern seems to have been laid down by *The Spanish Tragedy*, wherein, when Hieronimo's wife '*runs lunatic*,' her ravings are grandiose, formal, and operatic (III. viii). This is true of her husband in the original version, as of

Greene's frenzied protagonist in *Orlando Furioso*, and of all stock pre-Shakespearean madmen. But it is a far cry from Hieronimo's vein of plangent lamentation to the anonymous passages added later in a tersely modulated prose. These additions, notably the Painter's Scene, render the moods and changes of derangement far more vividly than Kyd's stilted pentameters, and may well register the influence of *Hamlet* on the revision of the older work. Credit for the actual innovation should be accorded to Marlowe's *1 Tamburlaine*, wherein the distraught Zabina anticipates Ophelia with a good-night speech in distracted prose (IV.ii.247–56).[6] Prose, with its pedestrian functions, is inherently a comic idiom, whereas the tragic note is traditionally sounded in verse. When the two modes converge, the result is what neo-classical critics of the Elizabethans deplored, the intermingling of hornpipes with funerals. For the romantics, it was the special glory of Shakespeare to unite the grotesque with the sublime, to catch the complexities of mixed emotion. The paradoxical hints in the opening speech of Claudius, 'mirth in funeral . . . dirge in marriage' (I.I.12), are poignantly acted out in the graveyard and in Ophelia's mad scenes, where snatches of ribald balladry make their subconscious comment on unfulfilled love. 'Thoughts and remembrance fitted' lend pertinence to her unshaped use of speech, while the symbolism of the flowers sets up a series of personal associations, making her case history 'a document in madness' (IV.V.178–9).

Similarly, blank verse breaks down into fragmentary prose, which compulsively recapitulates the psychological situation, in the somnambulism of Lady Macbeth or the delirium of King Lear. The latter has two companions in aberration: the half-witted Fool, whose prose is half-crazy, half-comic, and Edgar impersonating Tom of Bedlam. That impersonation had living models which Edgar describes (II.iii.13–20), as well as a dramatic forerunner in Diccon the Bedlam, or Vice, of *Gammer Gurton's Needle*. Furthermore, Edgar seems to have worked up his imprecations from a pamphlet by Samuel Harsnett on popery, just as Doll Common in Jonson's *Alchemist*—when she is supposed to be crazed by religious fanaticism—reels off a memorized page or two from Hugh Broughton's scriptural prophecies. This is an easier way of playing insane than Hamlet's, since he is compelled to sustain both sides of his dual role. Up to the end of the First Act, when the Ghost teaches him the grim lesson he writes upon his tables—the difference between *seems* and *is* as personified by the hypocritical Claudius—Hamlet speaks blank verse in all sincerity and sanity. Thereafter, as he warns Horatio and Marcellus in 'wild and whirling words,' he is to undergo a transformation (I.v.133). Throughout the rest of the play, until his feelings come to the surface again in the last act, his medium for dialogue is his own kind of antic prose. The exceptions to this rule are consistent: the soliloquies and his confidential interviews with Horatio and the Queen. Characteristically he shifts into verse when the others leave the stage:

> Ay, so, God b' wi' ye.
>
> *Exeunt* ROSENCRANTZ *and* GUILDENSTERN.
>
> Now I am alone.
> O what a rogue and peasant slave am I! . . . (II.ii.575–6)

Conversely, when he and Horatio are joined by the others, he maneuvers a quick change into prose:

> They are coming to a play. I must be idle.
> Get you a place.
>
> KING: How fares our cousin Hamlet?
> HAMLET: Excellent, i' faith; of the chameleon's dish. I eat the air, promise-crammed. You cannot feed capons so.
> (III.iv.95–8)

And Claudius is forced, against his habit, to continue more or less in Hamlet's medium. Hamlet forces the same shift upon his interlocutors in both the Fishmonger Scene and the Schoolfellow Scene. It also occurs at a crucial point in the Nunnery Scene, where, since he has been soliloquizing, and since he almost trusts Ophelia, he prolongs his greeting to her in verse. The fact that he switches with 'Ha, ha! Are you honest?' supports the argument that he has just then caught a glimpse of the skulking Polonius (III.i.103). Consequently Hamlet's distrust of Ophelia is confirmed; and henceforth he will address her too with bitterly cynical gibes.

Prose, for her, will give voice to authentic madness. He employs it for his histrionic escapade, though he finds it useful for other purposes when 'the wind is northerly' (V.ii.99): to parody the affectation of Osric, or to speculate on the human condition in language which moves from Florio's Montaigne toward the King James Bible. The main effect is to isolate Hamlet from everyone whose discourse runs in the expected rhythms, so that we are continually and painfully reminded of his exceptional predicament. Since the implicit distinction between the exterior and the inward man is marked in much the same fashion by Shakespeare's fellow playwrights, especially Marston, we may regard the device as a convention. As such, it is thrown into sharp relief in *The Malcontent*, where the titular character, Malevole, is actually Duke Altofront in disguise. With his confidant, Celso, he may talk in blank verse; but at the entrance of an old courtier who resembles Polonius, the stage-direction reads: '*Bilioso re-entering, Malevole shifteth his speech*' (I.i.255). What he says in prose is 'halter-worthy' yet privileged. 'He is free as air; he blows over every man' (I.i.42). Yet his railing is merely a source of amusement to the corrupted courtiers. It is significant that Malevole, like Hamlet, like most of Marston's heroes, and like so many protagonists of Jacobean drama, is a disinherited prince. Elizabethan heroics were exerted, more characteristically, to gain a crown; but disinheritance is the typical posture, and courtly intrigue the conventional plot, from the last years of Elizabeth's reign—with their disillusionment over the downfall of Essex—to the closing of the theaters and the dethronement of the Stuarts at mid-century.

The *maladie du siècle* was that self-conscious melancholy which even Jonson's gulls made a point of cultivating, which Shakespeare's Jaques exhibited so complacently—and so invectively, since it protected his sensibilities with the weapons of satire, keen and critical. Malevole-Altofront is a satirical commentator, as well as a princely revenger; under the former aspect he has much in common with Asper-Macilente in *Every Man in his Humour*, and with the other spokesmen of Jonson's Comical Satires. The stage—the stage that Hamlet walked—had become, in the reverberating phraseology of Davies of Hereford, 'a soiled glasse. . .'

> Where each man *in* and *out of*'s humour pries
> Upon himselfe, and laughs untill he cries.[7]

Shakespeare did not hold himself altogether aloof from this notorious War of the Theaters. *As You Like It* amiably satirizes the would-be satirist; *Troilus and Cressida* sounds the abysmal depths of detraction. *Hamlet*, which is closely related to these two plays in its composition, goes out of its way to take note of the controversy between the child actors and the public troops. The book that Hamlet reads, or so he professes, was composed by a 'satirical rogue' (II.ii.198). Because it appears to reflect against old men, it has been identified with the Tenth Satire of Juvenal. But Hamlet's conclusion, that crabbed age goes backward, is more suggestive of Erasmus' devastating paragraph on second childhood in *The Praise of Folly*.[8] Whoever the rogue may have been, the innuendo is lost on Polonius, perplexed as he is by the method in Hamlet's madness. Such 'pregnant . . . replies' have 'a happiness' that reason could hardly attain. Possibly they bear some resemblance to those 'happy unhappy answers' with which the comedian Tarlton used to make Queen Elizabeth laugh.[9] Hamlet's pithy repartee becomes more grimly enigmatic and less politely ironic, increasingly rude to his enemies as the play progresses. He becomes a master of the trope that rhetoricians defined under the heading of *sarcasmus:* Susenbrot's '*iocus cum amaritudine*,' Puttenham's 'bitter taunt,' Peacham's 'dispytefull frumpe.' [10]

Now Hamlet disapproves of comedians who attract attention by speaking 'more than is set down for them' (III.ii.43). Yet his own performance *ad libitum*, during the presentation of the play-within-the-play, is aptly compared by Francis Fergusson to the improvised antics of a 'night-club entertainer.'[11] In his manic phase, after the success of the entertainment, Hamlet momentarily toys with the notion of turning actor; and he displays the showman's aplomb when, by acting out the object-lessons of the recorder and of the cloud, he tells off Rosencrantz, Guildenstern, and Polonius. He does not put them out of their humors, in the Jonsonian sense; nothing short of their deaths, in just consequence of their deceptions, will accomplish that end. Rather, he indulges his own humor—and that of the audience; for, as the other Johnson pointed out, 'the pretended madness of Hamlet causes much mirth.'[12] Too many subsequent Hamlets, perhaps, have tended to overemphasize the solemnity of the part. After all, the pseudo-lunatic is conventionally a figure of comedy, which tends to bring out idiosyncrasies of character through its very appeal to social norms. A classic instance is the misplaced twin, in the *Menaechmi* of Plautus, whose bewilderment gets temporarily diagnosed as insanity. His exact symptoms reappear not only in *The Comedy of Errors* (IV.iv. 53–4) but also in Ben Jonson's *Silent Woman*

(IV.iv.56–8). They are aggravated in *Twelfth Night*, when Malvolio is confined and examined. But when Menaechmus was treated as a madman, he ended by living up to the accusation, insulting his brother's wife and father-in-law as Hamlet insults Ophelia and Polonius.

> Quid mihi meliust, quam quando illi me insanire praedicant,
> ego med adsimulem insanire, ut illos a me abstergeam? (831–2)

In reverse order Hamlet goes through those motions; and when he takes off his antic disposition, in the Closet Scene, it is difficult for him to convince Gertrude that he is sane. Both positions could easily be reduced to a comic level: the plight of the man who is generally misunderstood and the pose of the man who deliberately invites misunderstanding. *Hamlet* abounds in what—if it were an Elizabethan comedy—might have been designated as *errors* or *supposes*, misconceptions contrived and coincidental. Even the Ghost raises the question of a possible disguise, and Polonius dies a martyr to mistaken identity. Such questions could not be resolved by a happy ending, as they are in the first part of Dekker's *Honest Whore*, where a visit to an Italianate Bedlam clears up both the feigned madness of Bellafront and the suspected madness of Candido. We attain the *reductio ad absurdum* in the underplot of Middleton's *Changeling*, which also takes place in a madhouse; there the changeling, who counterfeits a madman because he is in love with the doctor's wife, discovers that a fellow inmate is a rival doing the same thing for the same reason. With the lady joining the masquerade, the lunatics and pseudo-lunatics dance 'a wild distracted measure,' which counterpoints the serious plot and completes the title's parallel between loss of mind and change of heart. A similar dance in Webster's *Duchess of Malfi* is supposed to exercise a homeopathic effect upon the melancholia of the Duchess. This treatment, in Ford's *Lover's Melancholy*, is elaborated into a masque, wherein the *dramatis personae* systematically represent the types that Burton had recently analyzed in his *Anatomy of Melancholy*.

By this time, the early Caroline period, the complaint is epidemic. 'Our commonwealth is sick. . . ,' declares an adviser of the bookish prince in *The Lover's Melancholy*, 'The court is now turned antic, and grows wild' (II.i.553–7). Contemplating 'the madness of the times,' a reduced courtier wonders, 'Why should not I . . . be mine own antic?' (I.i.251–4). And he proceeds to condense his worldly wisdom into an aphorism:

> He that pursues his safety from the school
> Of court, must learn to be madman or fool. (I.i.258–9)

This is a narrower choice than that between folly and knavery, which had so often confronted the protagonists in Jacobean tragedies of revenge. They usually chose as does Vindice-Piato in *The Revenger's Tragedy:*

> And therefore I'll put on that knave for once,
> And be a right man then, a man o' the time;
> For to be honest is not to be i' the world. (I.i.101–3)

Accordingly he plays the double agent, the revenger who becomes a villain in the very process of revenging the villainy he has been taught. But, since he has a genuine score to pay off, he is less completely villainous than Webster's agents, who seem to be disaffected intellectuals, Iago-like malcontents whose professional cynicism operates under a protective coloring of Hamlet-like prose. 'I do put on this feigned garb of mirth,' hisses Flamineo in *The White Devil*, 'To gull suspicion' (III.i. 30–31). In short, it is axiomatic with Hamlet's successors that the honest man can hardly survive to perform his mission at court, unless he disguises his personality with a mask of some sort, preferably foolish; the more outspoken he is, the better it suits him to be—like Feste in *Twelfth Night*—'an allow'd fool' (I.v.101). Hamlet, indeed, has an immediate predecessor, the exiled son of the Duke of Genoa in *Antonio's Revenge*, who literally dons a fool's habit and blows soap-bubbles. For his apologia he resorts to a commonplace as ancient as Aeschylus: 'He is not wise that strives not to seem fool' (IV.i.25).[13]

Antonio's self-justification, 'This coxcomb is a crown,' has its Shakespearean counterpart in the mockery of Jaques: 'Motley's the only wear' (II.vii.34). Jaques himself does not put on the coxcomb or motley; he wistfully envies the conversational liberties that Touchstone's professional garb allows him to take. Between Touchstone and Jaques, between the fool and what Hamlet would call 'the humorous man' (II.ii.334) there seems to be a special affinity, as there is between Passarello and Malevole in *The Malcontent*.[14] A similar relationship is presented, by Chapman in *A Humorous Day's Mirth*, between Labesha, the fool who repines against fortune, and Dowsecer, the young moralist in love. Hamlet, in his virtual isolation, differs from other humorous men; and unlike King Lear, he is not companioned by a fool. Yet the play, like the others that Shakespeare was writing at this period, has its fool's part; and, in view of its pervasive concern with death, it seems appropriate that this particular fool should have been dead and buried for three-and-twenty years. The skull that—in lieu of a coxcomb—personifies Yorick, the late king's jester, has become a mark of identification for Hamlet; it quickly became a standard property in plays like *The Honest Whore* and *The Revenger's Tragedy*. Since Yorick is a *muta persona*, whose gibes and gambols and songs are conspicuous by their silence, they are anticipated by the riddles and gags and equivocations of the Clown as First Gravedigger. The Prince plays straight man to him, eliciting—for the benefit of Shakespeare's English audience

—the remark that Hamlet's madness will not be noticed in England: 'There the men are as mad as he' (v.i.169).

What follows, when the clown identifies Yorick, is the gloomiest of recognition-scenes. The fool's traditional function has been to demonstrate that the other person, whatever his pretensions to wit may be, is likewise a fool; their dialectic, be it erratic or subtle, inevitably terminates with *tu quoque*. Here, however, the poles of the argument are no longer wisdom and folly but life and death. After rushing from his interview with Gertrude to hide the body of Polonius, Hamlet had diverted his conversation from the carnal to the charnel. He had responded to queries about his victim with a political pun on the Diet of Worms and a metaphysical conceit about royal flesh successively feeding a worm, a fish, and a beggar (IV.iii.32–3). That speculation will be exemplified in his sorites on Alexander and his lines upon Caesar (v.i.230–9), just as the generalizations about mortality will be brought home with shocking concreteness by Ophelia's funeral. Contrary to Hamlet's impression, the Gravedigger had some feeling for his business when he sought to lighten it by singing the song entitled 'The Aged Lover Renounceth Love.' Meanwhile, in the mode of Lucian speculating over the skulls and bones of Greek heroes and heroines, Hamlet satirically evokes the wasted lives of politicians, courtiers, and other ranks of society.[15] He summons them, as it were, to a dance of death, which culminates in the evocation of Yorick; whereupon, to Hamlet's *ubi sunt?* the death's-head replies *tu quoque*. 'Now get you to my lady's chamber, and tell her, let her paint an inch thick, to this favour she must come' (214–15). Hamlet's meditation thus develops the metaphor that Richard II adumbrates, when he personifies Death as 'the antic'[16] who scoffs and grins at the pomp of kings (III.ii.162).

In *Der bestrafte Brudermord* there is a live jester who bears the illusory name of Phantasmo; while in the *moralité* of Jules Laforgue, Yorick appears as Hamlet's elder half-brother; but, with Shakespeare, Yorick's role is posthumous. Hence, in his mortal absence, his former playfellow wears the comic mask. Hamlet, like Robert the Devil in the legend, becomes a court jester. He is not one to suffer other fools gladly; the very word sets the keynote for his relations with Polonius; and if Rosencrantz does not comprehend him, it is because 'a foolish speech sleeps in a knavish ear' (IV.ii.24–5). On the other hand, he can complain to Horatio, 'They fool me to the top of my bent' (III.ii.400–401). The sight of the apparition makes us 'fools of nature' (I.iv.54), even as—for the dying Hotspur—life is 'time's fool' (V.iv.81) and Romeo himself is 'fortune's fool' (III.I.141). So Hamlet, at the court where he cannot be king, must perforce be fool, an artificial fool pretending to be a natural. His assumption of foolishness is the archetypal feature of his story, as it has come down from primitive legend. In fact, his name derives from the Old Norse Amloði, which means 'a fool, a ninny, an idiot'—and, more especially, a Jutish trickster who feigns stupidity.[17] His Latin chronicler brings out analogies between his adventures and those of the Roman Brutus, whose name is also indicative of the brutal guise under which he must conceal his wiles.[18] Shakespeare, in refining upon such raw materials, utilized his mastery of those conventions which made the fool so strategic a figure on the Elizabethan stage.[19] The comment of Gilbert Murray is penetrating: 'It is very remarkable that Shakespeare, who did such wonders in his idealized and half-mystic treatment of the real Fool, should also have made his greatest tragic hero out of a Fool transfigured.'[20]

A fool transfigured or else a wise man denatured; for Murray might well have gone on to note that Hamlet is re-enacting the classical *eiron*, the Socratic ironist who practices wisdom by disclaiming it. More immediately, Shakespeare was dramatizing the humanistic critique of the intellect, as it had been genially propounded by Erasmus, to whom life itself was a kind of comedy, wherein 'men come foorthe disguised one in one arraie, an other in an other, eche plaiying his parte . . . And all this is dooen under a certaine veile or shadow, whiche taken awaie ones, the plaie can no more be plaied.'[21] When Hamlet, after playing hide-and-seek, is captured and brought in attended by guards, his self-humiliation seems complete: the noble mind overthrown, the capability and godlike reason thwarted by animal passion. But we should not forget that he is stooping to folly in the grand Erasmian manner, and that self-criticism is a premise which enables him to criticize others. 'The fool doth think he is wise,' in the saying of Touchstone, 'but the wise man knows himself to be a fool' (v.i.33–5). The advantages of this viewpoint, as originally eulogized in the *Encomium Moriae*, were versified by Jonson for the misbegotten chorus of his *Volpone*:[22]

> Fools, they are the only nation
> Worth men's envy and admiration . . .
> E'en his face begetteth laughter,
> And he speaks truth free from slaughter. (I.ii.66–7, 74–5)

Hamlet's complexity is compounded of many simples: the frustrated scholar, the unwilling courtier, the mourner who becomes a revenger, the lover whose imagination rages like that of the lunatic or the poet, and still others—not least, the witty fool. If he has the saturnine temperament, that accords with Ficino's vindication of gloomy genius. Why melancholy men are the wittiest is an inquiry which long ago evoked Aristotle's curiosity.[23] Democritus Junior, who subsumes all such ideas and takes the greatest pains to distinguish among them, conceives his subject as the occupational malady of the intellectuals;

and yet, he admits, such contagion is universal. 'For indeed who is not a fool, melancholy, mad?—*Qui nil molitur inepte*, who is not brainsick? Folly, melancholy, madness are but one disease . . . ' To sum it up in a pertinent question: '. . . . what madness ghosts us all?'[24] Against this context of prevailing unreason, Hamlet stands apart, a solitary sane individual in—shall we say, with Middleton?—*A Mad World, my Masters*. Or should we say, with Dame Purecraft in *Bartholomew Fair*, for whom the madman Troubleall is the one man of principle in a concourse of knaves: 'The world is mad in error, but he is mad in truth' (IV.iv.159–60). To that extent, the madness of Hamlet has its parallels in the maladjustment of Don Quixote, the misanthropy of Alceste, and the idiocy of Prince Myshkin.[25]

NOTES

1. Sir Israel Gollancz (ed.), *The Sources of Hamlet* (London, 1926), p.193.
2. Friedrich Gundolf, *Shakespeare und der Deutsche Geist* (Godesberg, 1947), p.31.
3. The most recent and comprehensive discussion is that of Lawrence Babb, *The Elizabethan Malady: A Study of Melancholy in English Literature from 1580 to 1642* (East Lansing, 1951).
4. Stéphane Mallarmé, *Divagations* (Paris, 1922), p.371.
5. R. R. Read, *Bedlam on the Jacobean Stage* (Cambridge, Massachusetts, 1952), p.5.
6. By the time of *A New Way to Pay Old Debts* (1633), this convention seems to have come full circle; Sir Giles Overreach raves in Marlovian blank verse.
7. John Davies of Hereford, *Complete Works,* (ed.) A. B. Grosart (Edinburgh, 1878), II, 76.
8. *The Praise of Folie,* tr. Sir Thomas Chaloner (London, 1549), B iv; see also F ii.
9. Quoted from Thomas Fuller by Enid Welsford, *The Fool: His Social and Literary History* (London, 1935), p.282.
10. T. W. Baldwin, *William Shakespere's Small Latine and Lesse Greeke* (Urbana, 1944), II, 144–5.
11. *The Idea of a Theater* (New York, 1953), p.134.
12. *The Plays of William Shakespeare,* ed. Samuel Johnson (London, 1765), VIII, 311.
13. Cf. *Prometheus Bound,* 1, 387.

14. E. E. Stoll, 'Shakespeare, Marston, and the Malcontent Type,' *Modern Philology* (June, 1906), III, 3, 1–23. Other scholars have not accepted Professor Stoll's early dating of *The Malcontent*, but they have not discredited his emphasis on the role.

15. *Dialogues of the Dead*, XVIII.

16. 'Antic' is here a substantive meaning *buffoon*, according to Schmidt, whereas Hamlet uses it as an adjective which means *fantastic*. However, Hamlet's usage carries an overtone of the buffoon's part he is about to assume. The three wayfarers in Peele's *Old Wives' Tale* are respectively named Antic, Frolic, and Fantastic. From the fact that the first drops out of the dialogue, it is to be inferred that he takes a leading part in the play-within-the-play.

17. J. V. Jensen, 'Hamlet,' *The London Mercury* (March, 1925), XI, 65, 510–11.

18. Gollancz, *op. cit.*, 28–33.

19. This view, essentially a renewal of Johnson's, was reasserted by the dramatic critic John Corbin in his Harvard undergraduate honors essay, *The Elizabethan Hamlet: A Study of the Sources, and of Shakespeare's Environment, to Show that the Mad Scenes Had a Comic Aspect now Ignored* (London, 1895). Later studies, delving more deeply into Shakespeare's background, tend to confirm the thesis of Corbin's subtitle.

20. *The Classical Tradition in Poetry* (Cambridge, Massachusetts, 1927), p.213. Cf. Wolfgang Clemen, *The Development of Shakespeare's Imagery* (London, 1951), p.110.

21. *Op. cit.*, E iii^{v}.

22. Cf. Harry Levin, 'Jonson's Metempsychosis,' *Philological Quarterly* (July 1943), XII, 3, 231–9.

23. The texts of Aristotle and Ficino are reprinted by Erwin Panofsky and Fritz Saxl in *Dürers Melencolia I: eine quellen- und typengeschichtliche Untersuchung* (Leipzig, 1923), pp. 93–120.

24. Robert Burton, *The Anatomy of Melancholy*, ed. A. R. Shilleto (London, 1893), I, 39, 46.

25. Another approach to the problem, via the convention of the Vice, has been taken by Sidney Thomas in *The Antic Hamlet and Richard III* (New York, 1943).

SUPPLEMENTARY STUDIES

THE TRAGIC ETHOS

[This review of *Hamlet: Father and Son* by Peter Alexander (Oxford, 1955) is here reprinted because it touches upon certain broader approaches to characterization and theory of tragedy.]

THe scope of this fresh and provocative study is belied by the misplaced concreteness of its title. Granted that the father-son relationship is fundamental to *Hamlet*, and that *Hamlet* is the most problematic play ever written by Shakespeare or by any other playwright, the problem raised and illuminated here is at once more specific and more general. It starts from a particular reading of a certain passage; but, before Peter Alexander has rounded out his commentary, he has touched upon some of the largest questions within the concentric spheres of esthetic theory and ethical thought. He has pertinently chosen his subject to fit his occasion—the delivery of the Lord Northcliffe Lectures at University College, London, in 1953. He has found an area of discussion near at hand and yet very widely extended, 'a common reference point' between the Shakespearean scholar and the public audience, in the recent film production of Sir Laurence Olivier. Focusing therefore on *Hamlet* in its most popular manifestation, Professor Alexander is open-minded but by no means uncritical. He has the courage to begin by diverging from Granville-Barker, for whom interpretation was presentation. It has taken more bookish Shakespeareans many generations to understand the controlling importance of stage performance; now that such understanding has been reached, there may be some danger of overemphasis; and it may indeed prove salutary to reaffirm, with Hamlet himself, the ascendancy of the poet over the player.

Professor Alexander's point of reference reminds us, at the very outset, that the theatrical interpreter is also indebted to the literary critic; for Olivier's *Hamlet* opens with a subtitle announcing that we are about to witness the tragedy of a man who could not make up his mind. This, of course, is an all but discredited commonplace of romantic criticism, based rather more on the introspection of Goethe and Coleridge than on the actual behavior of Shakespeare's protagonist. On the screen, however, it is supported by a caption quoted from the play, some dozen or sixteen lines which are usually cut in acting versions, beginning

> So oft it chances in particular men
> That, for some vicious mole of nature in them . . .

and ending, quite opportunely, just before the precarious 'dram of e'il.' Professor Alexander does not go on to criticize the film in any detail; if he did, he would doubtless concede that it does not live up to its professed conception of an ineffectual hero; on the contrary, it plays up the action so flamboyantly and abridges the contemplation so relentlessly that the figure of Hamlet coalesces with the lamented image of Douglas Fairbanks. But Professor Alexander is after bigger game than Sir Laurence. The aim of this 'friendly controversy' is nothing less than to reconsider—and possibly to refute—that tangled series of critical assumptions, involving 'The Substance of Tragedy' and 'The Heroic Tradition,' which find a locus in the cited speech.

It is not hard to put the speech back into its context, where it fills in a suspenseful period of watching and waiting for the Ghost (I.iv.23–36). Hamlet is generalizing about the tendency of human beings to generalize; and in this case the line of generalization proceeds from the alcoholism of Claudius to the repute of the Danes abroad, and toward the notion that characters otherwise admirable may suffer condemnation through

> the stamp of one defect,
> Being nature's livery, or fortune's star.

These sententious observations apply, in some measure, to all men; insofar as they can be applied to Hamlet, they may retrospectively be tinged with dramatic irony. Furthermore, loose and frequent citation has not only laid them down as a basis for Hamlet's own character but constructed thereon a whole ethos of tragedy. The defect that Hamlet mentions has been equated with the Aristotelian concept of *hamartía*, and Shakespeare has been claimed as an exponent of the classical doctrine that tragic retribution is the invariable consequence of some inherent moral flaw. That view, which receives its standard exposition in S. H. Butcher's treatise on the *Poetics*, is today a moot question among classicists, and has long been challenged by Ingram Bywater's alternative rendering in terms of mistaken judgment. *Hamartía*, as Aristotle described it, merely qualifies heroic perfection—and perhaps acknowledges Plato's suspicion that art was unheroic. Even for Aristotle's chief example, Sophocles, its significance has been recently minimized in a penetrating revaluation by Cedric H. Whitman.

All too many of Shakespeare's commentators have, in this respect, played the part of Job's comforters. Rather than face the problem of evil, the timeless fact that good men often suffer, they have scrutinized Shakespeare's heroes for defects which would justify their misfortunes and reaffirm the providential workings of cosmic design. Wishfully, they have presupposed that man is both the master of his fate and an object of supervision on the part of the gods, to a much greater extent than either science or theodicy would encourage us to believe. Hence the analysis of Shakespearean drama has taken a somewhat casuistic turn, and has compounded neo-Hegelian rationalization with quasi-Aristotelian terminology. The leading proponent of this eclectic method has been A. C. Bradley, toward whose superimpositions Professor Alexander is respectful but clear-sighted. He might have reinforced his cogent argument by appealing *a fortiori* to Thomas Rymer, whose very attack upon Shakespeare was based on his own moralistic concern for poetic justice: Desdemona's handkerchief was the notoriously insufficient cause of her suffering. In combating the influence of such preconceptions, Professor Alexander surrounds his discussion with an imposing and enlivening range of authorities, from Saxo Grammaticus to Raymond Chandler and from Werner Jaeger to Sir Donald Tovey. But for his more positive efforts, 'the works of Shakespeare viewed in their historical relationships' comprise 'the only relevant evidence.' Reading them in the dry light of a naïve Elizabethan didacticism, regarding their protagonists as self-condemned 'slaves of passion,' he would reject as pseudo-historical.

In shifting the emphasis from *hamartía* to *areté*, from the detection of the hero's faults to the admiration of his virtues, and especially to the central effect of catharsis, Professor Alexander equilibrates a theme which has been conspicuous for the one-sidedness of its previous interpretations. It is not surprising that those have tended to oscillate from one extreme to the other, given the basic polarity of the play. Scholars have sometimes attributed this to a cleavage between primitive material and sophisticated treatment; men of letters, notably T. S. Eliot, would discern some sort of obstacle between the dramatic medium and the dramatist's private emotions. Professor Alexander locates the conflict, where it surely belongs, in the characterization of Hamlet himself. Where else would the pale cast of thought wrestle with the native hue of resolution? Even Hamlet's original chroniclers wondered whether to present him as a paragon of wisdom or of bravery. By allowing then for a union of opposites, the interplay of contrasting emotions within a single magnanimous temperament, Professor Alexander resolves the intrinsic contradiction. It is a subjective resolution, which accords with the findings of modern psychology as well as with the insights of Dostoevsky and Proust. As for the objective issue, 'there is a conflict between new exigencies and old pieties,' between a humanistic present and a heroic past, concretely embodied in the obligations that the young intellectual of Wittenberg has inherited from the old soldier of Elsinore. 'The play dramatizes the perpetual struggle to which all civilization that is genuine is doomed'—man's need 'to be humane without loss of toughness.'

Thus, while suggesting a psychological framework worthy of *Hamlet's* unique complexity, Professor Alexander broadens its renewed meaning for our time. One cannot but wish that some of his thoughtful suggestions had been more precisely formulated and more fully elaborated; yet, by his somewhat glancing approach to the play, he has managed to take side-glances in several other important directions; and to wish he had said more, about a series of topics already so thoroughly canvassed and so extensively discussed, is high commendation. If an occasional sentence looks more awkward in print than it must have sounded on the platform, the book retains also the lecturer's animation, his unflagging pedagogical common sense, and his pithy anecdotal Scottish humor. Though its organization is discursive, its excursions are never irrelevant; they cover a good deal of ground and always come home, with a new pertinence, to the fundamentals. It is more than twenty-five years since Professor Alexander re-examined the bad quartos of Shakespeare's histories; and though the disintegrators have lately been re-emerging from the rocks, their Geiger-counters have not disclosed any serious rifts in his solid contribution to textual scholarship. Now, in the parallel field of interpretative criticism, he has again cleared densely obstructed ground. In the pseudo-science to which the Germans have given the dismal name of Hamletology, nothing is more needed than clarification. What Professor Alexander's monograph did for the integrity of *Henry VI* his present lectures may well do for the unity of *Hamlet*.

SUPPLEMENTARY STUDIES

AN EXPLICATION OF THE PLAYER'S SPEECH

[This paper is the result of an invitation from the University of Rochester, through whose permission it is now reprinted, to demonstrate a method of explication as applied to Shakespeare's *Hamlet*. The following lines were selected for that purpose, partly because of their unusual style, and partly because of their unique relationship to the play itself, to the Elizabethan theater, and to the Renaissance background. Though they have been detached from their context and renumbered for the reader's convenience here, they accord with the text of G. L. Kittredge, from which all other Shakespearean quotations below are cited. For a digest of earlier interpretations of the passage, see the Variorum Edition of H. H. Furness. Some of the more technical problems it raises have been surveyed by Else von Schaubart in 'Die Stelle vom "Rauhen Pyrrhus" in ihren Verhaltnis zu Marlowe-Nashes "Dido,"' *Anglia*, LIII, 4 (December, 1929). The standard works of Bradley and Chambers have been helpful in this connection, as in so many others pertaining to Shakespeare. I am also indebted for several illuminating sidelights to A. C. Sprague's *Shakespeare and the Actors* (Cambridge, 1944) and T. W. Baldwin's *William Shakspere's Small Latine and Lesse Greeke* (Urbana, 1944). Two further studies, too recent for utilization, should be mentioned here for the broad perspectives in which they place the theme of *theatrum mundi:* the seventh chapter of E. R. Curtius' *Europäische Literatur und lateinisches Mittelalter* (Bern, 1948), and Jean Jacquot's '"Le Théâtre du monde" de Shakespeare à Calderon' in the *Revue de littérature comparée*, XXXI, 3 (July-September, 1957).]

1 The rugged Pyrrhus, he whose sable arms,
2 Black as his purpose, did the night resemble
3 When he lay couched in the ominous horse,
4 Hath now this dread and black complexion smear'd
5 With heraldry more dismal. Head to foot
6 Now is he total gules, horridly trick'd
7 With blood of fathers, mothers, daughters, sons,
8 Bak'd and impasted with the parching streets,
9 That lend a tyrannous and a damned light
10 To their lord's murther. Roasted in wrath and fire,
11 And thus o'ersized with coagulate gore,
12 With eyes like carbuncles, the hellish Pyrrhus
13 Old grandsire Priam seeks. . . . Anon he finds him,
14 Striking too short at Greeks. His antique sword,
15 Rebellious to his arm, lies where it falls,
16 Repugnant to command. Unequal match'd,
17 Pyrrhus at Priam drives, in rage strikes wide;
18 But with the whiff and wind of his fell sword
19 Th'unnerved father falls. Then senseless Ilium,
20 Seeming to feel this blow, with flaming top
21 Stoops to his base, and with a hideous crash
22 Takes prisoner Pyrrhus' ear. For lo! his sword,
23 Which was declining on the milky head
24 Of reverend Priam, seem'd i' th' air to stick.
25 So, as a painted tyrant, Pyrrhus stood,
26 And, like a neutral to his will and matter,
27 Did nothing.
28 But, as we often see, against some storm,
29 A silence in the heavens, the rack stand still,
30 The bold winds speechless, and the orb below
31 As hush as death—anon the dreadful thunder

32 Doth rend the region; so, after Pyrrhus' pause,
33 Aroused vengeance sets him new awork;
34 And never did the Cyclops' hammers fall
35 On Mars's armour, forg'd for proof eterne,
36 With less remorse than Pyrrhus' bleeding sword
37 Now falls on Priam.
38 Out, out, thou strumpet Fortune! All you gods,
39 In general synod take away her power;
40 Break all the spokes and fellies from her wheel,
41 And bowl the round nave down the hill of heaven,
42 As low as to the fiends! . . .
43 But who, O who, had seen the mobled queen . . .
44 Run barefoot up and down, threat'ning the flames
45 With bisson rheum; a clout upon that head
46 Where late the diadem stood, and for a robe,
47 About her lank and all o'erteemed loins,
48 A blanket, in the alarm of fear caught up—
49 Who this had seen, with tongue in venom steep'd
50 'Gainst Fortune's state would treason have pronounc'd.
51 But if the gods themselves did see her then,
52 When she saw Pyrrhus make malicious sport
53 In mincing with his sword her husband's limbs,
54 The instant burst of clamour that she made
55 (Unless things mortal move them not at all)
56 Would have made milch the burning eyes of heaven
57 And passion in the gods.

(II.ii. 472–541)

I

THe text before us is a purple passage, not because it has been admired, but because it stands out from the rest of the play. On the whole it has aroused, in Shakespearean commentators, less admiration than curiosity and less curiosity than bewilderment. Some of them, like Polonius, have been quite frankly bored with it; many of them, unlike Hamlet himself, have considered it highly bombastic. Those who discern the hand of another playwright, whenever Shakespeare's writing presents a problem, have fathered it upon Marlowe, Chapman, Kyd, and even unlikelier authors. Others, hesitating to assume that Shakespeare would cite a fellow playwright at such length, have interpreted the speech as parody or satire—although who is being parodied, or what is being satirized, or how or why, is again a matter of diverging opinion. Still others have explained the incongruity, between these high-pitched lines and the ordinary dialogue, by assuming that Shakespeare had taken occasion to foist upon his patient audience a fragment of his earlier journeywork. As Guildenstern says of that theatrical controversy which accounted for the presence of the Players at Elsinore: 'O, there has been much throwing about of brains.' More rigorous scholarship tends to support the integrity of Shakespeare's text, just as more perceptive criticism emphasizes the consciousness of his artistry. Appealing to the authority of Sir Edmund Chambers, as well as to the insight of A. C. Bradley, we can proceed from the assumption that the passage at hand is both authentic and advised. But is it well advised? is it really significant? and what, if so, does it signify?

We can scarcely become aware of its significance without some preliminary awareness of its context: not only the intrinsic place that it occupies within the dramatic economy of *Hamlet,* but the stream of extrinsic associations that it carries along with it into the drama. The player who, at Hamlet's request, gives us this demonstration of his professional skill, this 'taste' of his 'quality,' is cast in a functional role; for in the next act he and his fellows are destined to perform the play that will 'catch the conscience of the King.' Meanwhile Shakespeare, who seldom misses an opportunity to talk about his craft, indulges in two of his fullest discussions on the theater. These are often regarded as digressions, and one of them is usually cut on the stage. There is indeed a ludicrous German adaptation which, omitting the Player's speech altogether, transfers the name of its protagonist, Pyrrhus, to the character of the King (*alias* Gonzago) in the play-within-the-play. But Goethe, who took a producer's point of view, saw how that 'passionate speech' served a psychological purpose by planting the suggestion in Hamlet's mind that leads to his experiment upon Claudius. And the late Harley Granville-Barker, perhaps the most pragmatic of all Shakespeareans, observed that the name of Hecuba was not only a necessary link between the First Player's scene and Hamlet's ensuing soliloquy, but also an implicit commentary on the Queen. To underline that observation: if the Player is nothing to Hecuba, or she to him, it follows *a fortiori* that Hamlet should feel and show a much deeper grief, and that Gertrude has failed abysmally to live up to the standard of royal motherhood.

What attracted Hamlet to this particular selection, from a play which he presumably had witnessed at its single performance, is as easy to understand as why he mentions Jephtha to Polonius. It is harder for modern readers to square his description of it with the specimen from it that follows; though the lines are said to contain no 'sallets' and the matter no affectation, the style is heavily conceited and the subject undeniably sensational. Yet Hamlet's famous excuse for the play's indifferent reception (' 'twas caviary to the general') runs curiously parallel to the publisher's complaint that *Troilus and Cressida* was 'never clapper-clawed by the palms of the vulgar.' The latter play is intimately linked to the fragment from *Hamlet* by their common theme, as well as by the turgid phrases and nervous rhythms that run through both. Coleridge, following A. W. Schlegel as usual, and followed by Bradley as usual, described the phraseology that Hamlet applauded as 'the language of lyric vehemence and epic pomp, and not of the drama.' Dryden, whose attitude toward poetic diction was rather more prosaic, distinguished between 'true sublimity' and what, in this instance, he labeled 'the blown puffy style.' He tried to deal gently with Shakespeare by denying him the authorship of the tirade, which he quoted as 'an example of expressing passion figuratively.' And, being rather more than a closet dramatist, he realized that the lines in question were not undramatic but melodramatic: '. . . to say nothing without a metaphor, a simile, an image, or description, is, I doubt, to smell a little too strongly of the buskin.'

However contrived, such contrivance lends an epic sweep to Shakespeare's more restricted medium. By requesting the account of 'Priam's slaughter' as it was told in 'Aeneas' tale to Dido,' Hamlet refers us to what might be called the official version: the retrospective story that Vergil tells in the second book of his *Aeneid* (506–58). This material, which the Earl of Surrey had utilized when he first experimented with English blank verse, was rendered more or less straightforwardly by Marlowe and Nashe in their early tragedy, *Dido, Queen of*

Carthage. But *Dido* does not seem to have influenced *Hamlet:* the single possible echo that editors note is based on a problematic emendation of Marlowe's text (II.i.254). Further and closer scrutiny of Shakespeare's treatment reveals that—although he elaborated a few small Vergilian details, such as the useless sword ('*inutile ferrum*')—he is actually less indebted to Vergil than to his favorite among the Latin poets, Ovid. When Lucentio pretends to be a schoolmaster in *The Taming of the Shrew* (III.i.27–37), he offers Bianca an unblushingly free translation of a couplet describing Troy from Ovid's *Heroides* (I.33–4). When literary narration supplements the bloody action of *Titus Andronicus*, Aeneas' tale to Dido is twice evoked (III.ii.27–8; V.iii.80–87); but then, when the schoolboy alludes to the madness of Hecuba, the book he happens to drop is Ovid's *Metamorphoses* (IV.i.20–21). Now it so happens that this very poem includes an unforgettable account of her metamorphosis (XIII.488–575), and that the relevant extract figured in Elizabethan schoolbooks as a stock example of 'copiousness'—that is to say, variety of expression in conveying emotion.

In shifting his attention from Priam to Hecuba, and his source from Vergil to Ovid, Shakespeare turns from the sphere of the epic to the lyric, and from events to emotions. It is Ovid, too, who inspires his final appeal to the gods themselves: '. . . *illius fortuna deos quoque moveret omnes.*' But the lyrical note can prevail no more than the epical, since Shakespeare's form is basically tragic; and here his classical model is indicated when Polonius, introducing the Players, warns: 'Seneca cannot be too heavy . . .' From 'English Seneca read by candlelight,' according to Thomas Nashe, playwrights were lifting handfuls—or were they *Hamlets?*—of 'tragical speeches.' These were couched in what Bottom the Weaver calls 'Ercles' vein, a tyrant's vein,' the vein touched upon by Shakespeare's Player when he conjures with fortune, darkness, blood, and hell. The tone of his speech is that of the *nuntius*, the Senecan messenger who enters to make a morbidly protracted recital of bad news from offstage—or, for that matter, the Sergeant in *Macbeth* (I.ii.8–42), whose sanguinary report makes the merciless Macdonwald a blood brother to the rugged Pyrrhus. Among the disheveled heroines of Seneca's tragedies, Hecuba looms particularly large as the archetype of maternal woe and queenly suffering. How she was metamorphosed into a dog, after the destruction of Troy, is recollected when, in Seneca's *Agamemnon*, she 'barketh as a bedlem bitch about her strangled chylde.' The *Troades*, in which she enacts the leading role, is one sustained lamentation, from the death of Priam to the sacrifice of their youngest daughter, the last of Pyrrhus' victims. The Elizabethan translator, pointing the moral, interpolates a chorus of his own:

> If prowes might eternity procure,
> Then Priam yet should live in lyking lust,
> Ay portly pompe of pryde thou art unsure,
> Lo learne by him, O Kinges yee are but dust.
> And Hecuba that wayleth now in care,
> That was so late of high estate a Queene,
> A mirrour is to teach you what you are
> Your wavering wealth, O princes here is seene.

Since the Elizabethans conceived of tragedy as a spectacular descent from the heights to the depths, they could conceive of no more tragic worthies than the King and Queen of Troy. Hence the object-lesson of the first English tragedy, *Gorboduc*, is driven home by identifying the heroine with '*Hecuba*, the wofullest wretch / That euer lyued to make a myrrour of.' And in the most popular of all Elizabethan plays, *The Spanish Tragedy*, the hero, instructing a painter to 'shew a passion,' volunteers to pose for his portrait 'like old *Priam* of *Troy*, crying: "the house is a fire . . ." ' But tragedy was more than a sad story of the death of kings and the weeping of tristful queens; it chronicled the fall of dynasties, the destruction of cities, the decline of civilizations. One of the set-pieces in Richard Rainolde's manual, *The Foundacion of Rhetorike* (1563), is entitled 'What lamentable Oracion Hecuba Queene of Troie might make, Troie being destroied.' European culture, looking backward, looking eastward, looking beyond Greece itself, saw its themes embedded in the primary myth of the Trojan War, and deduced its origins from the historic dispersion that underlay the mythological tradition. Hence even *Hamlet*, which is so deeply rooted in northern saga, has its classical moments: its cross-references to Caesar, Nero, Alexander, to Hercules, Hyperion, Niobe, above all to Pyrrhus, Priam, and Hecuba. Something was rotten in the state of Troy. Hamlet's fellow student at Wittenberg, Marlowe's *Doctor Faustus*, went characteristically farther: into that Gothic atmosphere he projected in the Mediterranean vision of Helen of Troy. Shakespeare caricatured it in *All's Well That Ends Well* (I.iii.74–5), rang changes on it in *Richard II* (IV. I.281–6), and exorcized it in *Troilus and Cressida* (II.ii.81–3). To convert the myth into explicit drama was to break its spell, as Thomas Heywood proved in *The Iron Age* by dramatizing the carnage that Shakespeare narrates and thereby reducing it to absurdity.

The matter of Troy—which Caxton had popularized, which English ballads celebrated, which poets and artists could draw upon as freely as the matter of England itself—served Shakespeare most effectively by helping to frame his characters and outline his situations. It figured upon a tapestry, as it were, backing the literal episodes of English history with a deeper dimension. The conflict between the houses of York and Lancaster was inevitably viewed in the light of the struggle between the Greeks and the Trojans. The father who accidentally slays his son in *3 Henry VI* (II.v.120), like Northumberland when he learns of Hotspur's death in *2 Henry IV* (I.i.70–74), is bound to see himself in Priam's role. Similarly, the Roman mother in *Coriolanus* (I.iii.43–6) and the cursing wife in *Cymbeline* (IV.ii.311–12) associate their grief with Hecuba's. It is not surprising, then, that the impassioned father wants to be painted as Priam in *The Spanish Tragedy*, or that the outraged wife in *The Rape of Lucrece* seeks consolation in a painting of the siege of Troy, more especially in its depiction of Hecuba (1450–51):

> In her the painter had anatomiz'd
> Time's ruin, beauty's wrack, and grim care's reign . . .

When Lucrece surveys the picture, discovering in it a precedent for her sorrows, its dumbness stimulates her to become vocal and its flatness puts her feelings into iconographic relief (1492): 'Here feelingly she weeps Troy's painted woes.' In similar fashion, all occasions inform against Hamlet, who rediscovers his own plight in the verbal painting, the theatrical mirror of the Player's speech. The narrator, pious Aeneas, recalls him to his filial duty. The King, his father, like Priam, has been slaughtered. The Queen his mother, ironically unlike Hecuba, refuses to play the part of the mourning wife. As for the interloping newcomer—whether you call him Pyrrhus, Neoptolemus, or Fortinbras—he too is prompted by the unquiet ghost of his father, Achilles. His destiny, too, is to bring down the revenge of a dead hero upon the unheroic heads of the living.

II

But these apparitions hover in the background until the words are pronounced that summon them. In moving to the foreground, turning from the context back to the text, our first impression may accord with André Gide's comment: 'the meaning of the words is much less significant than the tone and manner of the lines.' This is a convenient assumption for one who faces the problems of translating *Hamlet* into French. Happily, since we are not faced with any choice between meaning and manner, we have only to observe what each contributes to the other. Our first observation, once the speech has been detached from the dialogue, is that metrically it seems somewhat more formal than the body of the play. The usual gauge of metrical informality is the proportion of lines that run over or terminate with an extra syllable: the quotient of *Hamlet* as a whole, both for enjambments and for feminine endings, is roughly twenty-three per cent. The run-on lines in this passage (nineteen per cent) are somewhat fewer than the norm, while the off-beat endings (twelve per cent) are hardly more than half the normal percentage. Since the development of the Shakespearean line tends toward an ever-increasing flexibility, the present piece might be relegated to an earlier period on prosodic grounds; but there are other reasons for supposing that Shakespeare here deliberately reverted to a more stilted meter, along with a more artificial tone. Though the cesural pauses are not irregular, the grammar marks them more strongly than the prosody. Out of thirteen sentences, five begin, and one ends, with the line; eight begin, and twelve end, in the middle of a line.

The pulsating effect of these cadences, turbulently beating against conventional restraints, is matched by the diction. A barrage of striking tropes and strained expressions overwhelms the reader or hearer immediately. But a second reading lays bare a basically simple vocabulary, a preponderance of familiar Saxon monosyllables over archaisms, neologisms, technical terms, and Latinate polysyllabics. Three of the lines are entirely monosyllabic (18, 41, 42), with what propriety we can best judge later. The strange words, however, are so far-fetched and so strategically placed that they diffuse their strangeness throughout. Ten of them do not occur elsewhere in Shakespeare: 'coagulate,' 'fellies,' 'hush' (as an adjective), 'impasted,' 'mobled,' 'o'ersized,' 'o'erteemed,' 'repugnant,' 'unnerved,' and 'whiff.' One of these, 'unnerved,' seems to be one of Shakespeare's many gifts to the English language. Several others, according to the New English Dictionary, were coined by this speech but never achieved much currency: 'impasted,' 'mobled,' 'o'ersized,' 'o'erteemed,' and the adjectival 'hush.' Such idiosyncratic language might provide an argument in favor of non-Shakespearean authorship, were it not counterbalanced at every point—as Bradley has shown—by thoroughly Shakespearean turns of phrase and thought. Even the false start that Hamlet makes at the outset has its significance: 'The rugged Pyrrhus, like th'Hyrcanian beast . . .' How that beast, the tiger, goes ramping through Elizabethan drama, as the proverbial embodiment of hardness of heart, a glance at any concordance will show. It cut a meaningful figure in the parting reproaches that Vergil's Dido brought against Aeneas; and, curiously enough, it supplied Robert Greene with an epithet to fling against Shakespeare himself.

After this understandable lapse, Hamlet starts out correctly, and now the cruelty of Pyrrhus is symbolized by his heraldic trappings. Knightly prowess ordinarily finds its outward symbol in armorial panoply, which is frequently contrasted with the reality of blood, sweat, and tears—notably in the characterization of Hotspur. Here, where that situation is reversed, bloodshed is treated as if it were decoration. The sable arms of Pyrrhus resemble his funereal purpose, and also the night—which is not a generic night, but the particular, portentous, claustral night that he and his companions have just spent in the wooden horse. The repeated adjective 'black' (2, 4) is an elementary manifestation of evil, like the 'Thoughts black' of the poisoner in the play-within-the-play; yet it hints at that 'power of blackness' which Melville discerned more fully in Shakespeare's works than anywhere else. But the scene does not appear in its true color until its dark surfaces are 'o'ersized' (11), covered with sizing, dripping with redness. Red, unrelieved by quartering, is 'total gules' in the unfeeling jargon of heraldry, which Shakespeare deliberately invokes to describe the clotted gore of others shed by Pyrrhus—of parents and children whose family relationships are feelingly specified by way of contrast (7), a contrast which ultimately juxtaposes esthetic and ethical values. He is tricked out, dressed up in the unnatural colors of Marlowe's Tamburlaine—in black and red and in a carbuncular brightness which flickers against the darkness, as opposed to the hues of nature, the blues and browns and greens that Shakespeare has more constantly in mind. Thence the metaphor shifts from light to heat, from visual to tactile images, and to a zeugma which holds in suspension both physical fire and psychological wrath (10). The impasted product of such infernal cookery bears a sinister resemblance to that Senecan pastry in which Titus Andronicus baked his victims.

At this point, the appropriate point where Pyrrhus encounters Priam, the Player takes up the story and—in a manner of speaking—the monologue becomes a dialogue. It should not be forgotten that 'anon' (13) is one of those adverbs whose force has been weakened by time: in this case it means 'very soon' rather than 'later on.' It reinforces the series of 'nows,' which in their turn reinforce the employment of the present tense, and convey the impression of breathless immediacy: we might almost be listening to the play-by-play account of a sporting event. The ineffectuality of the old grandsire's antique sword (15), whose fall prefigures his (19), is motivated by the spirit of general mutiny. The angry swing of his assailant—which, though it goes wild, deprives the father of his remaining strength, unnerves him—rends the air with ten onomatopoetic monosyllables: 'But with the whiff and wind of his fell sword . . .' (18). The doublet, 'whiff and wind,' like the apposition of 'bak'd and impasted,' is a twist of phrasing which recurs throughout the play: e.g., 'Th' expectancy and rose of the fair state.' And though the poet hesitates to indulge in a pathetic fallacy, to attribute sensation or sensibility to the city itself, he interprets the crash of its topless towers as a comment on the downfall of its king. Troy, however, has its momentary and metaphorical revenge upon Pyrrhus when the noise, by capturing his ear, arrests his motion. At that fatal moment everything stops; the narrative is transposed to the past tense; and the interjection 'lo!' (22) points a moral and pictorial contrast between the bloody tyrant and his 'milky' victim (23). Where Lucrece animated a picture with her grief, this episode makes pain endurable by reducing it to two dimensions and setting it in an ornamental frame. The art of painting, almost as frequently as the art of drama, is Hamlet's analogy for the hypocrisies of the court, the discrepancies between appearance and reality.

It is only during this uncharacteristic standstill that Pyrrhus, the unthinking avenger, shows any likeness to his polar opposite, Hamlet. Standing there for the nonce in a cataleptic state of neutrality, as if he had no control over mind or body, equally detached from his intention and his object, he 'did nothing'—and the pause is rounded out by an unfilled line (27). Then as he swings into action by way of an epic simile, sight is commingled with sound—or rather, with the absence of sound, since we are asked to visualize a silence (29). And as our gaze is deflected from the clouds to the earth, a second simile takes its departure from the first, and perceives an omen of death in the silent atmosphere (31). Anon—that is, suddenly—like the awaited thunderclap, vengeance is resumed; the retarded decline of the sword (37), with its Homeric reverberation

(34), now parallels the dying fall of Priam and of his sword. The word 'fall,' coming twice in pairs, accentuates the rhythm and underlines the theme. The classical allusion, a preliminary glimpse of 'Vulcan's stithy,' though somewhat archaically expressed, would be commonplace if it were not for the violence of Shakespeare's application. He uses a favorite stylistic device of his predecessors, the University Wits, who seldom made a comparison without making it invidious: their characters are more beautiful than Venus, as powerful as Jove, no weaker than Hercules. After all, there could be no more remorseless task than to beat out indestructible armor for the god of war. To display as little or less remorse, while striking down a disarmed graybeard, was to be as devoid of sympathy—as ready to inflict suffering and unready to feel it—as any human being could expressibly be.

Dwelling on gross details and imperfections of the flesh ('Eyes without feeling, feeling without sight'), Hamlet will admonish his mother that sense-perception is dulled by sensual indulgence. Here insensibility is communicated by a rhetorical assault upon the senses: primarily 'the very faculties of eyes and ears,' but incidentally touch and even taste. Leaving the senseless Priam to the insensate Pyrrhus, after another hiatus of half a line (37), the speech addresses violent objurgations to the bitch-goddess Fortune, about whom Hamlet has lately cracked ribald jokes with Rosencrantz and Guildenstern; whose buffets and rewards he prizes Horatio for suffering with equanimity; against whom he will, in the most famous of all soliloquies, be tempted to take arms. An appeal is addressed to the gods, who are envisaged as meeting in epic conclave, to destroy the source of her capricious authority. It is urged that her proverbial wheel, whose revolution determines the ups and downs of individual lives, be itself dismantled; and that its components suffer the destiny to which they have so often carried mortals—to fall, as the angels did in the world's original tragedy, from paradise to hell. To catch the gathering momentum of that descent, Shakespeare again resorts to words of one syllable (not excepting 'heav'n'), and relies—as he does throughout—upon assonances and alliterations (41, 42): 'And bowl the round nave down the hill of heaven/ As far as to the fiends.' The same image, that of 'a massy wheel,' disintegrating as it rolls downhill, is later likened by Rosencrantz to 'the cesse of majesty,' the death of the king involving 'the lives of many' attached to its spokes:

> . . . when it falls,
> Each small annexment, petty consequence,
> Attends the boist'rous ruin.

The fact that the twenty-three foregoing lines (19–42) are frequently omitted from acting versions, notably from the First Quarto, supports the view that they constitute a rhapsodic excursion from the narrative. Shakespeare cleverly obviated boredom on the part of his audience by allowing Polonius to complain and Hamlet to gibe at him. By laughing with Hamlet at Polonius, whose own tediousness is the butt of so many gibes, the audience is pledged to renew its attention. Hamlet, of course, has personal motives for echoing the Player's mention of Hecuba. Thereupon Polonius, who fancies himself as a critic, and who has said of Hamlet's letter to Ophelia that ' "beautified" is a vile phrase,' seeks to propitiate Hamlet by voicing judicious approval of a peculiarly inept expression: ' "Mobled queen" is good.' Has impressionistic criticism ever said more?

The barefoot queen remains mobled, or muffled, for better or for worse, in spite of editors who prefer 'mob-led' or 'ennobled.' Her special poignance depends upon her abdication of queenly dignity, upon the antitheses between 'diadem' (46) and 'clout' (45) and between 'robe' (46) and 'blanket' (48).

Shakespeare utilized 'blanket' for the very reason that Dr. Johnson sought to exclude it from *Macbeth:* because it degraded what it enveloped, its connotations were neo-classically low. It is also a prefiguration of the 'incestuous sheets,' the rumpled images of Gertrude's bed, which are constantly lurking in the morbid recesses of Hamlet's imagination. The concept of royalty has been debased: 'Hyperion to a satyr,' goddess to fishwife. The sword, on its fourth and last appearance, is not unlike a kitchen-knife; while the final outburst of Hecuba is like Homer's portrayal of Helen, in one respect if in no other, since it registers its emotional impact on the spectators. Fortune, it would appear, is still so securely entrenched that the impulse to denounce her is a poisonous subversion of things as they are (50). To appeal once more to the gods is to admit—more skeptically than Ovid—that they may exhibit an Olympian disregard for the whole situation: such is the question that Shakespeare explored in *King Lear*, and which such modern writers as Thomas Hardy have reconsidered. Yet if heaven takes any interest whatsoever in man's affairs, it might be expected to respond to so harassed an incarnation of feminine frailty, and its presumptive response inspires a last downward sweep of sinking metaphor. Its tears, burning like the lurid eyes of Pyrrhus, turning into milk like the revered hair of Priam, and associated by that maternal essence with Hecuba's 'o'erteemed loins' (47), might produce a downpour more blinding than her 'bisson rheum' (45) and thereby extinguish the holocaust of Troy. What commenced in firelight concludes in rainfall. Recoiling before this bathetic *Götterdämmerung*, Dryden remarks: 'Such a sight were indeed enough to have rais'd passion in the Gods, but to excuse the effects of it [the poet] tells you perhaps they did not see it.'

III

To break off the speech is to awaken Hamlet from what he calls 'a dream of passion'—a glaring nightmare of smoke and screams and ruins—to the light of day. But somber northern daylight renews 'the motive and the cue for passion' in his own life, and the Trojan retrospect becomes a Danish omen, joining the echoes of Caesar's assassination and other portents of Hamlet's tragedy. None of the others, however, could have seemed as epoch-making or epoch-shattering as the evocation of Priam, no less a byword for catastrophe to the Elizabethans than the name of Hiroshima seems to us. 'O what a fall was there, my countrymen.' The catastrophic mood that overtook sensitive Englishmen during the latter years of Elizabeth's reign, particularly after the downfall of Essex, had set the key for the play. From the long-echoing lament of Hecuba, as enunciated by Ovid, Shakespeare had learned the rhetorical lesson of copiousness. It is also probable that his books of rhetoric had taught him an old argument of Quintilian's: that the orator who pens his own speeches would move his hearers more profoundly than the mere elocutionist who recites what someone else has felt and thought and written. At all events, the surface of the drama is undisturbed by the Player's elocution. Again he is merely a player; Polonius is quite unaffected; and Hamlet completes his arrangements for the morrow's performance of the play that will affect Claudius as—it soon appears—this foretaste has affected him. Hitherto constrained from weeping or speaking his mind, he now reveals that the player has wept and spoken for him. The deeply revealing soliloquy that completes the Second Act and sets the scene for the Third, 'O what a rogue and peasant slave am I,' pulls aside the curtain of heavily figured declamation that has just been spread before us for that very purpose.

To be more precise, the soliloquy is the mirror-opposite of the speech. Both passages are very nearly of the same length, and seem to be subdivided into three movements which run somewhat parallel. But where the speech proceeds from the slayer to the slain, and from the royal victim to the queenly mourner, the soliloquy moves from that suggestive figure to another king and finally toward another villain. And where the speech leads from action to passion, the soliloquy reverses this direction. Where the Player's diction is heavily external, underlining the fundamental discrepancy between words and deeds, Hamlet's words are by convention his thoughts, directing inward their jabs of self-accusation. Midway, where the Player curses Fortune as a strumpet, Hamlet falls 'a-cursing like a very drab.' Well may he hesitate, 'like a neutral to his will and matter,' at the very point where even the rugged Pyrrhus paused and did nothing. Though we need not go so far as Racine, who refined that model of bloody retribution into the gallant lover of Andromaque ('*violent mais sincère*'), we may cite the precedent as a justification—if further justification still be needed—for Hamlet's often criticized delay. While he must hold his tongue, so long as he 'cannot speak' his genuine sentiments, the Player is vocal on his behalf. Since he is all too literally 'the observed of all observers,' he must enact a comedy and so must they: the courtly comedy of fashionable observance. He offers Rosencrantz and Guildenstern the same treatment that he accords the Players, to whom he also must 'show fairly outwards.' Polonius, who has acted in his youth, ends—all too ironically—as Hamlet's 'audience.' And while the courtiers watch Hamlet, he watches Claudius, the most subtle impersonator of them all, who conceals his villainy behind a smile and only reveals it while watching a dramatic performance.

Afterwards, when Hamlet confronts his mother with her 'act,' he undertakes to show her 'a glass/ Where you may see the inmost part of you.' The Elizabethan conception of art as the glass of nature was ethical rather than realistic; for it assumed that, by contemplating situations which reflected their own, men and women could mend their ways and act with greater resolution thereafter. To the observer who is painfully learning the distinction between *seems* and *is*, the hideous pangs of the Trojan Queen are the mirrored distortions of Gertrude's regal insincerities. The 'damn'd defeat' of Priam, reminding Hamlet of his father, prompts him to renounce his hitherto passive role, to soliloquize on the Player's example, and finally to evolve his plan of action. Thus his soliloquy departs from, and returns to, the theatrical sphere. 'The play's the thing'—the play-within-the-play, where the Player's 'passionate speech' will be crowned by the Play Queen's 'passionate action,' and the crime will be metaphorically ('tropically') re-enacted, beginning and ending with Hamlet's echoed quotations from two notorious tragedies of revenge. Meanwhile the situation at hand is transcended by the searching question in Hamlet's mind—a question which ponders not only the technique of acting, but the actual nature of the esthetic process. Why should the Player—'Tears in his eyes, distraction in's aspect'—have been carried away by the speech? Was he, like the Platonic rhapsode, literally inspired? Did he feel the part because he was well trained in what today would be known as the Stanislavsky method? Or would he sustain the paradox, which French philosophers have argued, that the most moving actor is the most cold-blooded hypocrite? 'What's Hecuba to him, or he to Hecuba, / That he should weep for her?' What is the relationship of the player to the play, of the dancer to the dance, of the work of art to its interpretation, or of the interpreter to the audience? How, Shakespeare asks himself in effect, can emotion be communicated by my dramaturgy?

Observe—and here I beg leave to reduce our text for the

moment to a paradigm (see Figure 3, page 168.)—that he does not present Hecuba's emotions directly. Her passion, unlike Thisbe's, is neither presented nor described. Instead he describes her appearance and appeals to the spectator: 'Who, O who,' he opines—or even more lugubriously, as the Quartos would have it, 'Who, ah woe!'—whoever viewed that spectacle would repudiate destiny itself. Thence the poet appeals the case to a higher court:

> But if the gods themselves did *see* her, then,
> When she [Hecuba] *saw* Pyrrhus make malicious sport,
> In mincing with his sword her husband's [Priam's] limbs—

even they (the GODS) might feel an emotional response, though such a prospect is conditionally stated. Let us meet the condition by recognizing their existence on a highly figurative plane, and by characterizing their attitude as *compassion:* a sympathetic participation in the feelings of Hecuba. They are not besought, as in *King Lear* (II.iv.275–81), to instill a vengeful animus. When Claudius subsequently hints at his devious purposes, Hamlet retorts that these are known to heaven: 'I see a cherub that sees them.' An ultimate vision is glimpsed as indirectly as the flicker on the wall of Plato's cave. The same double process of visualization and recognition works toward a different end, when Hamlet sees Claudius see the play. When Ophelia expresses Hamlet's plight and her own, she sums it up in a couplet which is her version of his 'O cursed spite!'

> O woe is me
> T' have seen what I have seen, see what I see!

Laertes, when he sees Ophelia's madness, will call the gods to witness; and Gertrude will be the witness—or, at all events, the choric narrator—of Ophelia's death. HECUBA is likewise an onlooker, tense though the bond of sympathy must be that unites her to the agonies of Priam; it is he who feels, who suffers physically when Pyrrhus acts. PYRRHUS is your man of *action,* in the most epical and extroverted signification of the term: the key to this passage is the emphasis that Shakespeare places upon his insensibility. Furthermore, no effort is made to present the sufferings of PRIAM: his falling city sympathizes with him, his animistic sword rebels against him, but he himself remains inanimate. Tradition depicts him slain upon the altar of Apollo, and—although Shakespeare makes no point of this circumstance—it sheds the light of religious ritual upon his sacrifice, and helps to explain why so many generations could identify it with their experience. In terms of sheer brutality, or ritualistic fulfilment, the murder might be regarded as a *passion,* and differentiated by an exclamation-point from the question-mark that might appropriately designate the psychological *passion* of Hecuba. But even the burden of her grief, as we have noticed, is relayed to higher authorities: if the gods exist and look down, perhaps their compassionate overview will gather up the vicarious passions of the dead Priam, the unfeeling Pyrrhus, and the muffled queen. And we are left confronting a dizzying hierarchy of externalized emotion, which continues to refer our query upwards until it is out of sight.

Let us therefore look in the other direction, downwards—from the eyes of the gods, past Hecuba and the murderer and the murdered, to the voice of the narrator. When all is said and done, we must not forget that it is AENEAS who speaks: a surviving eye-witness who relives the tale as he tells it to Dido. Since she is not represented, its impact on her goes unregistered. But since the epic has been adapted to the drama, *narration* has become *action* in quotation-marks, simulated actuality; while Aeneas is enacted by the PLAYER. Shakespeare exploits the ambiguity of the verb 'to act,' which alternates between 'doing' and 'seeming,' between the brutal deeds of Pyrrhus and the verbal hypocrisies that Hamlet dwells on: 'For they are actions that a man might play . . .' By means of his acting, the Player simulates *passion*, again in quotation-marks; he functions as a surrogate for the various mythical figures whose respective sorrows he personifies, and bridges the gap between their world and Hamlet's. David Garrick, as HAMLET, attempted to strengthen this understanding between them by the dubious business of pantomiming the Player's words. The scene's effectiveness depends precisely upon the differentiation between their passive and active roles. The Player need not 'tear a passion to tatters,' but neither should he be 'too tame,' and under latter-day stage direction he is likelier to err by domesticating verse into drawing-room prose. Simply to 'suit the action to the words' is, in this instance, to be something of a Termagant. And who could be histrionic with better right than a Shakespearean actor acting an actor? Hamlet's expressed distrust of histrionics, on the other hand, lends an air of naturalness to his own behavior: hence, according to Partridge in *Tom Jones*, Garrick as Hamlet is not much of an actor, while anybody may see that the King is really acting. Furthermore, this natural Hamlet must put on an 'antic disposition,' must from time to time assume a mask of madness which derives significance from whatever distinction he manages to establish between his real and his raving selves. Even now, in the constraining presence of Rosencrantz and Guildenstern and Polonius, he has started to rehearse. And the Hamlet who consequently emerges from inaction can—and on occasion does—out-Herod the players, challenging Laertes to mouth and rant in the vein of *Hercules Furens*, and recounting his sea-adventure as if it were a play. Within a few years his name will already become such a byword for theatricalism that, in a poem on *The Passion of Love* by Anthony Scoloker, the lover 'Calls Players fooles . . . Will learn them Action . . . Much like mad-*Hamlet;* thus a Passion teares.'

Since the theater perforce exaggerates, amplifying its pathos and stylizing its diction, it takes a specially marked degree of amplification and stylization to dramatize the theatrical, as Schlegel realized. Conversely, when matters pertaining to the stage are exhibited upon the stage, to acknowledge their artificiality is to enhance the realism of everything else within view. The contrasting textures of the Player's fustian and Hamlet's lines, like the structural contrast between the prevailing blank verse and the rhyming couplets of the play-within-the-play, bring out the realities of the situation by exposing its theatricalities. By exaggeration of drama, by 'smelling a little too strongly of the buskin' in Dryden's phrase, Shakespeare achieves his imitation of life. Yet the play itself—not 'The Murder of Gonzago' but *The Tragedy of Hamlet, Prince of Denmark*—is 'a fiction,' an illusion which we accept on poetic faith. Hamlet's passion is sincere and sentient as compared to the Player's, which—though externalized and factitious—has aroused Hamlet from passivity to action. And of course he is not, in the very last analysis, 'passion's slave'; he is, he becomes, an agent of revenge; he suits 'the word to the action.' Nor is he a recorder to be played upon, though he succeeds in playing upon Claudius. The implied comparison with Aeneas would be completed by Dido's counterpart in the neglected person of Ophelia, but dalliance in either case is resolutely cut off. When Hamlet hits upon his ingenious plot, it projects him in two directions at once: back to the plane of intradramatic theatricals, and forward to the plane of his audience. A spectator of the players, he has his own spectators, who turn out to be ourselves, to whom he is actually an ACTOR. Here we stand in relation to him—that is, to his interpreter, be he Garrick or Gielgud—where he stands in relation to the Player. The original emotion, having been handed down from one level to another of metaphor and myth and impersonation and projection, reaches the basic level of *interpretation*, whence the expression can make its impression upon our minds. There the reality lodges, in the *reaction* of the AUDIENCE: the empathy that links our outlook with a chain of being which sooner or later extends all the way from the actors to the gods.

Shakespeare's appeal to his audience, like Orlando's to the Duke Senior in *As You Like It* (II.vii.117), is always made on the basis of common experience: if we are expected to sympathize, it is because we 'know what 'tis to pity and be pitied.' On the dramatist's side, his insight into character—which the eighteenth century termed 'sympathetic imagination'—is concretely based upon his ability to enter into many different lives and to respond, vicariously yet whole-heartedly, to all the situations they encounter. If tragedy induces pity and fear, we must also remember that Aristotle defined pity as fear lest the fate of others overtake ourselves. Asking us to put ourselves in Hamlet's—or Hecuba's—place, Shakespeare stages a series of emotional displacements all along the line. His willingness to share her unhappiness, across so many removes, and even to question the ways of providence as manifested toward her, finds its polar opposite in the fable of La Fontaine (X.13), where the object-lesson is viewed in relatively comfortable detachment:

> Quiconcque, en pareil cas, se croit haï des Cieux,
> Qu'il considère Hécube; il rendra grâce aux dieux.

That remote Hecuba, the *ne plus ultra* of misfortune, and therefore a properly qualified exemplar of the consolations of philosophy, is still significant, still archetypal within the literary frame of reference. The failure of modern literature to maintain a relationship with her and what she represents is the failure of modern life to sustain human relationships, as Aldous Huxley interprets them in *Antic Hay*. There, to the syncopated rhythm of the foxtrot and the modulated timbre of the saxophone, our Shakespearean theme is given what may well be a final variation:

> What's he to Hecuba?
> Nothing at all.
> That's why there'll be no wedding on Wednesday week,
> Way down in old Bengal.

The marriage of minds, as Shakespeare arranges it, admits fewer impediments. If now and then it turns actors into virtual spectators, there are reciprocal occasions on which the spectators are virtually turned into actors. When Hamlet, glancing excitedly in three directions, says:

> I have heard
> That guilty creatures, sitting at a play,
> Have by the very cunning of the scene
> Been struck . . .

we shift in our seats uneasily, wondering whether there may not be a Claudius in the house. Audience-participation engenders what might be termed a play-outside-the-play. It is hard to see how Shakespeare's original Gravedigger, speaking of Hamlet's voyage to England, could have kept from winking at the English groundlings when he said: 'There the men are as mad as he.' Elizabethan drama is full of such interplay between the stage and the pit, as well as the tiring-house. Playwrights were not less conscious of their medium than Pirandello or Tieck. For Shakespeare, whose world was a stage and whose theater was the Globe, life itself could be 'a poor player,' the best of actors could be 'but shadows,' and Hamlet's ambition could be 'the shadow of a dream". Of the roles that the playwright may have played himself, we hear of two in particular, one of them the Ghost in *Hamlet*. It has been traditional for the actor who plays that role to double as the First Player. May we not suppose, without straining conjecture very far, that it was Shakespeare who first delivered the Player's speech; and that he is speaking expressly, through its rhetorical configurations, of how poetry accomplishes its effects?

FIGURES

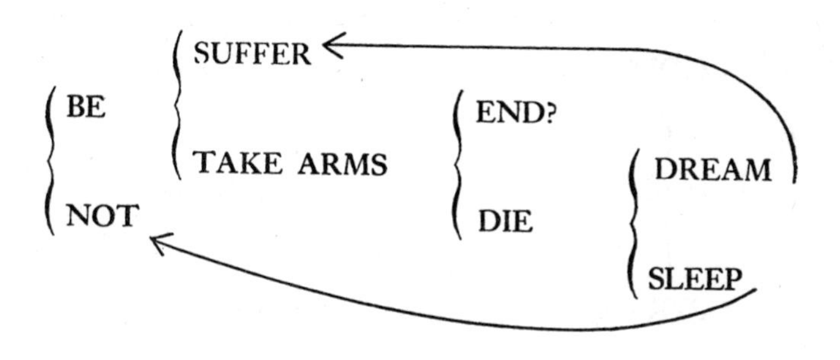

FIGURE 1

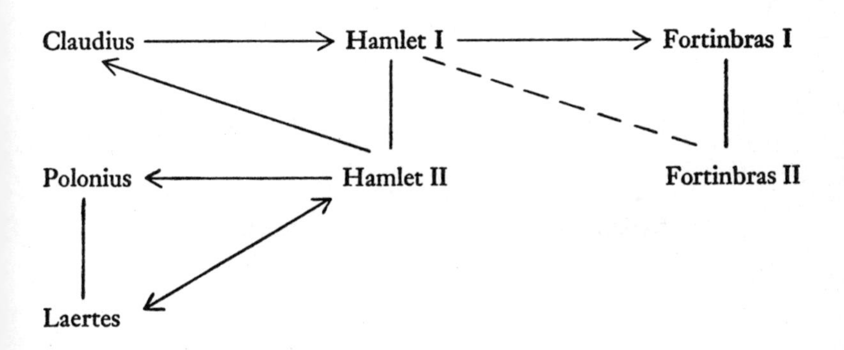

FIGURE 2

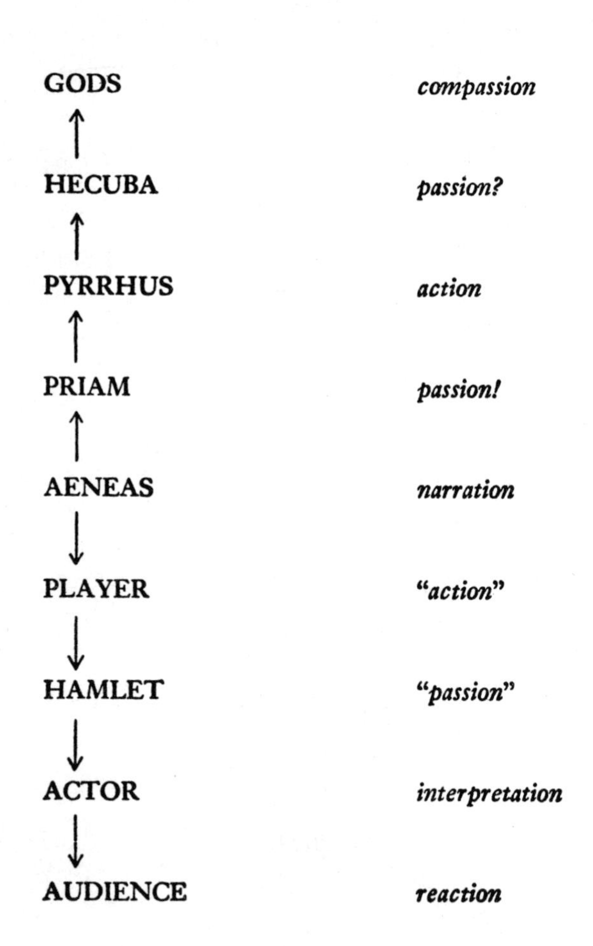
GODS
compassion
HECUBA
passion?
PYRRHUS
action
PRIAM
passion!
AENEAS
narration
PLAYER
"action"
HAMLET
"passion"
ACTOR
interpretation
AUDIENCE
reaction

FIGURE 3

INDEX

INDEX

LIST OF LINES CITED

LIST OF LINES CITED

Page-references are in parentheses